Teenagers and Technology

**Chris Davies and
Rebecca Eynon**

 Routledge
Taylor & Francis Group

LONDON AND NEW YORK

Published 2013
by Routledge
27 Church Road, Hove, East Sussex, BN3 2FA

Simultaneously published in the USA and Canada
by Routledge
711 Third Avenue, New York, NY 10017

Routledge is an imprint of the Taylor & Francis Group, an informa business

© 2013 Routledge

British Library Cataloguing in Publication Data
A catalogue record for this book is available from the British Library

Library of Congress Cataloging-in-Publication Data
Davies, Chris.
  Teenagers and technology/Chris Davies & Rebecca Eynon.
  p. cm.
  1. Internet and teenagers. 2. Internet – Safety measures. I. Eynon,
  Rebecca. II. Title.
  HQ799.2.I5D38 2012
  004.67′80835 – dc23   2012021673

ISBN: 978-0-415-68457-6 (hbk)
ISBN: 978-0-415-68458-3 (pbk)
ISBN: 978-0-203-07927-0 (ebk)

Typeset in Times New Roman
by Florence Production Ltd, Stoodleigh, Devon

MIX
Paper from
responsible sources
FSC® C004839
www.fsc.org

Printed and bound in Great Britain by
TJ International Ltd, Padstow, Cornwall

Contents

Acknowledgements

We would like to express our gratitude to all those who worked on the Learner and their Context project: Andrew Carter, Anne-Marie Chase, Sue Cranmer, Anne Geniets, Jenny Good, John Furlong, Melissa Highton, Isis Hjorth, Stuart Lee, Lars-Erik Malmberg, Jane Shuyska, Dimitrina Spencer; all those at Becta who helped to guide the project, especially Adrian Higginbotham; and most of all, the young people who talked to us about their lives and who, along with their parents and teachers, so generously enabled our work.

1 Opening

Introduction

In this book we examine the extent and ways in which new technologies are important in the lives of teenagers. This is a topic that has been frequently discussed in many contexts, too often in terms of unexamined generalities about the young that ignore the complexity and gradually changing nature of their participation in a shared digital culture. Popular discourse about this issue tends to assume a rich and rewarding relationship between young people and the technologies they use, to the extent that they are typically represented as the ideal beneficiaries of the digital era. The book will explore both the distinctive and specific ways in which new technologies do indeed have special meaning for teenagers as a broad group, and the ways in which that meaning varies a great deal for different young people, on occasions resulting in ambivalent and sometimes negative feelings about technology.

The notion of teenagers has particular resonance with regard to digital technologies. Much research, including our own, suggests that it is during the teenage years that young people most intensively develop, share and establish their own repertoire of technology-enabled activity, forming a set of practices that – though always to some extent in a state of flux – will remain with them through their studies and on into their working lives. The affordances of new technologies seem particularly pertinent to their needs and goals as people moving from the care and protection of their families towards the autonomy and self-determination of adulthood, and as a crucial means of establishing their own identity and membership of peer group sub-culture. At the same time the adult world is increasingly keen to impress upon young people somewhat contradictory reservations about the very same resources that are offered to them as essential to their future progress.

By new technologies, we mean both the hardware that enables access to digital resources and networks, and the uses of those resources and

networks. The key characteristics of technological devices that figure most in the lives of teenagers are increasingly those of convergence and multi-functionality: 'technology' refers to a range of digitally-encoded things that people want to do on whatever devices are available, as much as it does to the devices with which specific activities are more traditionally associated. Smartphones, tablets, laptops, netbooks and games consoles all offer scope for communication, networking, play, collaboration, learning, and many forms of making and consuming culture. The capacity to move easily from one activity to another, and do so on any number of different devices, constitutes the technology sub-culture that is supposedly available now to all young people. How they are actually engaging with such opportunities and that sub-culture at the current time is the focus of the book.

The picture is constantly changing, and therefore this book will not attempt any kind of summative account of the topic, so much as an overview of how things are at a time when constant engagement in networked technologies has become the norm for most young people in the developed world. Central questions that the book addresses are therefore: what does that normality of teenagers' technology use involve, is that normality common to most young people, and what are the implications for the significant numbers of young people who remain excluded from it? In order to explore such issues, we shall make wide reference to published writing, including studies of adolescence, youth studies and studies into young people's uses of technology in particular. Alongside this, we shall refer throughout to material from a substantial research project that we carried out between 2008 and 2011 in Britain. In the course of that project we talked with over 200 boys and girls (predominantly but not exclusively teenagers) as well as with some of their parents and carers, and surveyed over a thousand youngsters nationally (we describe this project in more detail below, on page 11). The book will draw extensively on what these young people told us, and will use their own words in order to help us build a picture of its core issues.

The book will therefore cover many aspects of teenagers' experience of technology: social networking and online engagement in their wider social world; building self-identity and group membership online; games-playing; developing technology skills; using those skills in support of their own learning; coping with issues of risk online, and drawing on technology resources to support their journeys towards adulthood. In the final section of this chapter, we show how these things will form the content of the rest of the book.

Before that, in the two following sections, we discuss the theoretical foundations underlying the two key notions around which this book is

written: first teenagers, and then technology. This is followed by an introduction to the research project upon which much of this book is based.

Teenagers

Adolescence and the teenage years is a period of life that is characterised by numerous biological, cognitive and social changes. It is a recognised life stage, which people pass through on the way to becoming an adult. The precise nature of this period and the perspectives people hold about it differ. Indeed, there are numerous competing positions on childhood and adolescence both in terms of disciplinary focus and ontological viewpoints (Wyness, 2012).

While there has been a fascination with children over centuries, the specific term teenager was first used after the Second World War in America. It was initially used to reflect a category of young people aged 14–18 for marketing purposes, highlighting a new market segment that had spending power and 'a group with its own rituals, rights and demands' (Savage, 2007: xiii). Now, of course, it is widely used as a common-sense term to represent those young people aged between 13 and 19.

The term adolescence has a longer history, established as a field of study in 1904 by Stanley Hall (Adams and Berzonsky, 2005). Stanley Hall's research on adolescence was primarily concerned with psychological processes, yet emerged at a time when concerns about youth delinquency were prevalent in wider society (Savage, 2007: xvi). Thus, from the beginning the inextricable link between biology and society was clear. As with the term teenager, most of us hold a common-sense view of what we mean by adolescence, typically associating it with the onset of puberty. In academic terms the definition is somewhat more contested, with differing views about when adolescence begins and ends, the relative importance of biological and social processes and if it encompasses one or multiple life stages (Coleman, 2011).

In this book we deliberately use the word teenager, and for the most part use age to make sense of this category. As will be seen in later chapters we use Steinberg's three broad phases of adolescence: early adolescence, from about 10 to 13 years old; middle adolescence, from about 14 to 18 years, and late adolescence, which might then continue into the early 20s (2002: 4). We recognise that age, on its own, cannot account for the significant variation in young people's physical, social and developmental circumstances (Coleman, 2008; Steinberg, 2002), but it is a relatively useful proxy to help us understand the various cognitive developments and contextual aspects of young people's lives that may

help us to make sense of their experiences. For example, at the age of 12 young people are just becoming very aware of social situations and contexts (Coleman, 2008), by 14 and in later adolescence the development of identity, a sense of agency towards educational institutions (both positive and negative) and the importance of peers becomes even more significant (Fine, 2004); by 17 young people are no longer in or nearing the end of compulsory schooling and have made or will soon make certain choices (e.g. about staying in formal education and/or starting a job).

We are not biologists or developmental psychologists, and so come to this discussion from more of a social and cultural perspective. In doing so we wish primarily to highlight the experiences of teenagers, but set this within a broader frame. As Larson suggests, research in this area needs to think both about 'adolescents (i.e. the immediate experiences of individual youth) and adolescence (i.e. the generalised patterns, norms, and expectations that affect what those individuals experience, including changes in the adulthood for which they prepare)' (Larson, 2002: 7–8). In the next two sections we review some of the literature from these two related perspectives.

Understanding individual experience

Until relatively recently, the majority of social science research viewed children and teenagers as the objects rather than subjects of research (Green and Hill, 2005). This began to change quite significantly in the 1960s, when there was a wider movement to recognise the voices of marginalised groups, including a more explicit acknowledgement of a child's position as a fully functioning member of society. This is neatly illustrated in the field of sociology, where the Sociology of Childhood paradigm was introduced in the 1980s (Corsaro, 2004; James and Prout, 1997). From this perspective children were viewed as a heterogeneous group, who were able to speak for themselves and the society of which they were part (Matthews, 2007).

This shift has led to more studies that aim to understand the experiences of what it is like to be a child or teenager using a range of methodologies to enable the individual's voice to be heard. As Green and Hill note, 'The researcher who values children's perspectives and wishes to understand their lived experience will be motivated to find out more about how children understand and interpret, negotiate and feel about their daily lives. If we accept a view of children as persons, the nature of children's experiential life becomes of central interest' (Greene and Hill, 2005: 3). This has been supported by policy-makers and

practitioners who have also sought over the last couple of decades to obtain children's and young people's perspective and voice in their decision-making (Greene and Hill, 2005).

Social life

Of course, these experiences do not operate in a vacuum. They take place in a social context, one which is supported and constrained by social structures such as the education system, gender inequalities, employment laws and practices, norms, stereotypes and expectations of the family and teenagers themselves. Teenagers interact with this world, thus both contribute to and are influenced by it. As Christensen and Prout note, 'rather than looking only at how children are formed by social life, children are seen as social actors whose actions can both shape and change social life' (2005: 50).

The nature of the society of which teenagers are part changes over time, and this has implications for the way that teenagers experience the world. In the industrialised West we see three conflicting trends: institutionalisation, where young people spend increasing amounts of time in formal spaces such as school and after-school clubs; familialisation, where young people are more economically dependent on their family, spend more time at home for leisure, and leave home older; individualisation, where teenagers are in some ways more independent – determining their identity through purchasing goods, using their newly acquired right for their voice to be heard and being less dependent on expert authority (Christensen and Prout, 2005: 50, citing Brannen and O'Brien (1995) and Nasman (1994)).

As we discuss in Chapter 3, the interaction of these trends leads to the adolescent years becoming longer, with young people starting work later (Coleman, 2011; Livingstone, 2009). Related to this are the consistent (and in some cases growing) inequalities within countries. In general, adolescents from better-off homes have improved opportunities to prepare for adulthood due to the availability of a range of resources (Larson, 2002), whereas those with multiple disadvantages (such as substance dependency, homelessness and being in care) have far less opportunities to prolong this period of their lives to help them with the transition to adulthood (Parry, 2006).

Also important here are the numerous tensions and contradictions teenagers experience due to these trends (Christensen and Prout, 2005; Livingstone, 2009). The trend of individualisation in some ways does not fit well with familiarisation. For example, teenagers live in a very consumerist culture, with marketers targeting them to choose purchases

that define their identity. Yet, these young people are still at school or have limited resources. Thus, the finances for these purchases typically come from parents. As Livingstone notes, 'parents must tread the difficult path between providing for their children economically for an extended period of time while simultaneously recognising their independence in terms of sociality and culture' (Livingstone, 2009: 6). Throughout this book we highlight a number of these kinds of contradictions in the world of teenagers. Technology in some cases enables certain kinds of freedom, yet this typically operates within a context that is characterised by the control and rules of others.

Like other researchers in this area (e.g. Christensen and Prout, 2005: 50), we believe that there is a need to understand both the experiences of adolescents and the wider, more macro trends and institutions in which these experiences play out. In understanding teenagers then, we try to understand the interaction between individual experience and wider society primarily through the eyes of young people. We try to place the teenagers' experiences at the heart of our discussions and to understand these within their local sub-cultures, and how they interact with and are informed by the interaction with wider social influences (Holloway and Valentine, 2000).

Technology

Drawing on the work of Arthur (2009), Jones (2012) suggests that technology is often used to reflect three different levels of analysis: technology as a tool; technology as part of a system; and technology at a society wide level. In simple terms, looking across the history of technology studies, it is possible to detect a continuum in the ways that people conceptualise technology across all of these levels, ranging from a strong form of technological determinism through to those that utilise perspectives from the social shaping of technology approach.

In many countries, the dominant discourse about technology tends to be relatively upbeat, with many seeing new technologies as something that offers society a great deal of opportunities for the individual and for society as a whole. Indeed for some, information and communication technologies are the defining feature of our times, making our world significantly different to the lives that have gone before (Dearnley and Feather, 2001; Robins and Webster, 1999). The excitement and hope around information and communication technologies has led to a belief in 'keeping up' with technology and a stress on the importance of harnessing its power in a range of contexts including in the lives of young people, to support their learning, to ensure they are equipped with the

necessary skills to become effective members of the workforce and to develop the necessary skills to protect them from the potential harms as well as the opportunities of technology.

The key problem with much of the debate, particularly in the domains of policy and the media, is the relatively deterministic assumptions that are made about information and communication technologies. This leads to a way of thinking and asking questions about technology that are too simple and couched in terms that are not necessarily helpful, that focus on impacts or effects rather than influences or experiences. Thus instead of thinking about the complexity of the interactions between the person, other people, the technology and the context, the focus is all on the technology and what it can do 'to' us – a highly instrumental focus that is apparent in a numerous policy areas (Friesen, 2009). It is generally accepted in the research community that any influence of ICTs will vary as a result of a range of complex and interrelating factors both at micro and macro levels (Dutton, 1996; Kling, 2000; Preston, 2001; Woolgar, 2002). Indeed, social shaping theories of technology emerged in the 1980s in response to a critique of technological determinism that was popular at the time (Williams and Edge, 1996; MacKenzie and Wajcman, 1985), and we take a similar view.

In debates about technology we also tend to forget the past, so that both policy-makers and researchers are sometimes guilty of reinventing the wheel and neglecting the insights from research and experiences of previous technologies (Caldwell, 2000; Jones, 2012; Selwyn, 2011). Historically, each new media technology tends to be associated with 'utopian projections about how they will transform humanity' (Flew, 2002: 55) and often similar dystopian ones too (Burnett and Marshall, 2003). We try hard in this book not to make a similar mistake. Here, then, what we try to do is to understand technology within the social, economic, cultural and political context of which it is part; and this applies to all three levels of technology outlined by Jones (2012). Crucially we are not interested in the effects that technology has on young people's lives but the way that they experience, use and think about technology as a part of their life: a life which is, as it always has been, characterised by biological changes, significant others, multiple expectations and numerous choices.

Why teenagers and technology?

As noted above, there is a clear link between our understandings of teenagers and the society of which they are part. When we look at the trends that may influence what it means to be a teenager now and in the

coming years, technology is likely to play an important role in at least some of them. In saying this we are not suggesting that we are in a radically new era, one that is fundamentally different from the past due to the impacts of technology (c.f. Webster, 2006). Yet society is constantly changing in a number of subtle ways over time, and these changes are likely to influence what it means or feels like to be a teenager, and the part that teenagers play in society. As Larson notes, 'there is every reason to believe that population growth, globalization, new technologies, and other fast moving changes will reconstruct the concept of adolescence again, in many forms' (Larson, 2002: 2).

These changes in society mean that our understandings of young people need to be constantly renegotiated and critically assessed. Indeed, Savage argues our understanding of teenagers now needs to be redefined as the American teen image from the 1950s still continues to dominate world views about young people (Savage, 2007). Thus part of our reason for writing this book is simply because it is important to study teenagers' experiences of technology given that they represent an important and significant segment of the population. Quantifying the sheer amounts of technology tells us little about what this actually means for people's lives (Webster, 2006), and we believe that there is a great deal to be gained from determining the nature and importance of these social changes in qualitative terms.

Enabling possibilities

One way of thinking about this question is through thinking about if and how technologies offer teenagers new ways of doing old things or, less commonly, taking advantage of entirely new opportunities.

As indicated above, the teenage years are characterised by transition(s). This is conceptualised in different ways. Initially research viewed adolescence as one transition, but over the past decade or so this has shifted. Some researchers support the notion of different kinds of transition, such as those related to school and lifestyle, in young people's attempts at working towards adulthood (Coles, 1995). Others, in line with Graber *et al.* (1996), maintain the view of adolescence as a single transition and instead highlight differing 'turning points' in a teenager's life that may incorporate positive or negative experiences. For example, the stress caused by delayed puberty or a poor fit between the individual and the new school they find themselves in (Coleman, 2011). While researchers cannot agree on the specific nature of these turning points or transitions, or the relative importance of them (Coleman, 2011), young people themselves are very much aware of this part of growing

up and tend to have a set of expectations and desires concerning these transitions that may or may not be reflected in reality (Parry, 2006).

Given that the majority of activities that young people engage in can be mediated by some kind of technology (Livingstone, 2009), it may be possible that for certain cases and for certain individuals, technology can facilitate or support particular transitions or turning points. Other potentially related opportunities may be particularly important in terms of social interaction. Indeed, for Jones (2011, 2012) emerging new technologies afford new types of social engagement, in part answering the question 'so what is new'?

Making meanings

Closely related to this issue is the need for research that goes beyond thinking about opportunities to look at implications. Thanks to a relatively large body of work in the past decade or so we now have a good deal of descriptive data about how teenagers use technology. It is now time to get below the surface of these descriptions, to see if using (or not using) the Internet and other new technologies a great deal constitutes a real problem (Livingstone, 2009). What does the use of technology really mean for teenagers' relationships, health, learning, participation and employment?

As noted above, we view technology as a layer that is interwoven and bound up with the experiences of being a teenager. Thus it is likely that sometimes in some contexts technology has importance for teenagers – but in others not so. We are not looking here for some kind of fundamental or groundbreaking shift in adolescence; rather we hope to present a more complex, subtle and nuanced story, but one that takes us beyond our current understandings. While surveys can tell us a lot about use, they are not strong on telling us about meaning. This is where the everyday experiences of individuals become more important (Oliver, 2012). In the context of education and technology research, Oliver argues for a more relational and situated approach to the study of technology 'where, technology can no longer be understood simply in terms of its functions, but has to be reconceived in relation to people, practices and purposes' (Oliver, 2012: 442). This is similar to the views we hold here.

Against anxieties and essentialism

Negative popular discourses about young people can be traced back to the ancient Greeks (Adams and Berzonsky, 2005; Smetana, 2011). More

recently, Jon Savage suggests that the period between 1875 and 1945 can be seen as a kind of pre-history of the teenager, when concerns about youth took place at a time when developed Western countries were changing significantly due to increased urbanisation, industrialisation and rearmament. At such times, young people may be used as a way to reflect wider societal concerns. As Livingstone comments, '"the child" or "childhood" has become a stand-in for something else – a means of articulating anxieties about Western capitalism. Often, these are debates about tradition, authority or respect for shared values, or about the balance between individualism and participation' (Livingstone, 2009: vii).

Technology increasingly plays a part in common discourses about teenagers. Like the examples above, these discourses take various forms: sometimes being quite negative, or taking a more anxious tone, or the complete opposite. Yet they all have something in common in that they tend to view the relationship between teenagers and technology in essentialist terms. Work from this tradition either puts forward a dystopian view where vulnerable children will be exploited by this technology or a utopian view where children, unlike adults, are seen as possessing a natural innate ability to use and excel at using technologies (Buckingham, 1998). Selwyn identifies six discourses about young people and new technologies in the UK prominent in media and policy circles since 1980 to 2000, all of which are in some way technologically, socially or biologically deterministic. These include: the 'natural' child computer user where children are seen as having an innate ability to use technology; the 'adult' child computer user where children are expert and teachers novices and young people have to show adults (in a non-threatening way) how to use technology; the 'victimized' child computer user where innocent young children are exposed to undesirable content (Selwyn, 2003: 355–66). These discourses can be seen as important in a broader economic and political sense, supporting both the commercial markets for new technologies as well as the implementation of IT government strategies (Selwyn, 2003).

Empirical research has presented a more fine-grained and balanced picture of how this supposedly homogenous generation actually engage with new technologies, especially in their own time, within their own settings (e.g. DiMaggio and Hargittai, 2001; Facer and Furlong, 2001; Livingstone and Helsper, 2007; Bennet *et al.*, 2008). Indeed, critiques of this discourse in respect to young people are not particularly new (e.g. Thurlow and McKay, 2003; McCay *et al.*, 2005; Brown *et al.*, 2008; Kennedy *et al.*, 2008; Helsper and Eynon, 2010; Jones and Ramanau, 2009). Yet, what is interesting is that despite empirical evidence to the

contrary, teenagers themselves seem to have to define themselves in relation to technology just like they have to define themselves in relation to other things, such as music or other cultural choices and the ways they dress, because these essentialist myths remain fixed in the public discourse.

In this book we do not consider that being a teenager is some kind of essentialist and easily defined state, but instead see it as something that is constructed and shaped by the culture and society around them (Matthews, 2007: 325). This is not to say that biological and psychological processes are not important, but mainly insofar as they interact with the social and cultural environment. While we do not put this book up as another critique of these essentialists' discussions (enough excellent work has been done on this already), we do wish to make it clear that we reject such popular views of teenagers and regard them more as a set of discourses that impinge on young people themselves and on the ways in which they see themselves.

As the above discussion recognises, there is a range of developmental, psychological, sociological and anthropological perspectives on children (Greene and Hill, 2005), with academics from different fields focusing primarily on one perspective with greater or lesser recognition of the others. From a disciplinary perspective, this book is relatively eclectic but tends to draw more on social psychology, sociology, education, mass communication and Internet studies than predominantly biological and developmental perspectives. Our intention is that we can connect our understandings of technology more closely with discussions of youth and adolescence.

The Research: *The Learner and their Context Project*

As mentioned at the start of this chapter, the comments and insights from teenagers that are quoted during the course of this book are drawn from research we carried out between 2008–2011, as part of *The Learner and their Context Project* funded (and named thus) by the UK government educational technology agency, Becta. Our project was one of several projects of research and development around the government's *Harnessing Technology Strategy*, with a particular focus on young people's 'experience outside formal education; learner voice; online subcultures; developments and trends in learners' behaviour and experience' (from the original call). We were thus in the happy position of needing to monitor and study teenagers' technology lives, the technologies they had access to, the things they did with these, and how these practices were developing and enabling them to cope, or prosper, in an increasingly

digital world. As time went on, the scope of the research expanded to include investigation into the opportunities for using technologies to support learning as experienced by vulnerable and unconnected learners such as Looked After Children, SEN learners and mainstream learners without regular access to the Internet at home. In doing so, we tried to address the challenges of representativeness in projects that are commonplace in studies similar to our own.

Such a wide-ranging focus required us to plan research that would enable comparison between learners within and across different age groups, in terms of access to technologies in their own contexts, nature of parental involvement, specific learning difficulties and challenges, issues of Internet safety and safeguarding, and the role of technology in supporting learners' progression through their educational careers and into the workplace. We utilised a wide range of data collection methods to do this, including one-to-one interviews, home visits and surveys. The one-to-one interviews with young people aged from 8–21 (the majority being teenagers) took place in primary and secondary schools, colleges, universities and homes: we spoke at length with over 200 young people, and in addition conducted a representative survey of over 1,000 more, during the course of these three years. Often many studies of childhood and children tend to be either macro or micro in perspective (Holloway and Valentine, 2000). In our own study we took a mixed method approach to try and gain different insights and benefit from a range of different perspectives.

The majority of interviews took place in and around the town of Reading, England with additional interviews carried out in the Midlands and east of London. The young people were drawn from a number of learning institutions purposively selected with the aim of including students with a range of demographic and socio-economic profiles. Initial interviews were designed to explore what young people do when they are able to use technologies away from their formal education settings: participants were encouraged to talk about what they liked to do in their free time, how technology fitted in with that, and the ways in which their own uses of technology made learning possible, in both formal and informal ways. Interviews lasted between 25 and 40 minutes depending on the age of the young person, and took place initially in their school, college or university. Roughly one third of these young people were interviewed again in each of the two succeeding years, in order to find out if and in what ways their experiences of using technologies had changed over time.

A selected number of those interviewed in their educational settings were subsequently interviewed in their homes, so that we could see the arrangements of their home technology use, what they did there, and how

that fitted into their family world and their developing lives as young adults. During these home visits, one researcher would speak to the young person about his or her normal use of a range of technologies with a particular focus on their use of the computer, and would ask him or her to give a step-by-step demonstration. A second researcher would speak at the same time with a parent or carer about their views on their children's technology uses.

This approach to some extent borrows from the extensive work that has been done in the field of education on learner voice (Fielding, 2001; Rudduck, 2006), in particular with respect to our beliefs that children and teenagers are quite capable from an early age to talk about important things in their lives (Furlong and Cranmer, 2009). That said, we were very much aware that our views and interpretations of the conversations was not necessarily shared by the teenagers we spoke to. Researching and understanding children and young people's experiences is a challenging task, due often to issues of power and the choices a researcher needs to make about their role in relation to their participants and how their participants perceive them (Greene and Hill, 2005).

All interviews were recorded and transcribed. Data analysis was carried out in accordance with the principles from the qualitative tradition. The analysis took place via three interrelated and circular stages of reducing the data: 1) coding, searching for patterns and identifying categories; 2) displaying the data (primarily via the use of tree diagrams and matrices); and 3) drawing and verifying the conclusions by noting similarities/differences and testing propositions (Miles and Huberman, 1994; Boulton and Hammersley, 1996). Through this analysis a number of key themes emerged that gave a greater insight into the core issues of the study. In the analysis of our data we were not utilising a logic of triangulation. Instead, we found the logic of crystallisation more valuable. In such an approach multiple forms of data help to put together different parts of the picture, but it is never satisfactorily complete (Ellingson, 2009). As Richardson notes,

> I propose that the central image for 'validity' for postmodern texts is not the triangle – a rigid fixed two dimensional object. Rather the central imagery is the crystal which combines symmetry and substance with an infinite variety of shapes, substances, transmutations, multidimensionalities, and angles of approach.
>
> (Richardson, 2000: 934)

Given the qualitative nature of much of this research, we do not suggest that the interview data can be taken as fully representative of the

entire population of young people in the UK, but we do think it is illustrative of a very substantial portion. The young people who participated in the research came from a wide range of homes and social situations, most belonging within the 85+ per cent of the population of learners in Britain who at the time of the research lived in Internet-connected homes (Eynon, 2009). As indicated above, we were able to supplement the insights from our interview data with the results of a fully representative nationwide survey conducted for us by a professional survey company, ICM, of 1,069 young people across the age range.

The focus of this survey was specifically on use and non-use of a range of different technologies and the individual and contextual factors that may help to explain this use. In particular, age, gender, attitudes and skills, quality of access to technology, and family, peer, school and work contexts were explored. The sample was identified using output areas (each comprising around 150 households) that were randomly drawn using the ACORN classification. In each of these output areas the interviewer was asked to find one 8 year old, one 12 year old, one 14 year old and one 17–19 year old to interview, knocking on every third door. All the young people included in the survey were interviewed at home by a researcher from ICM. Parents were welcome to be present during the discussion and in 56 per cent of cases a parent or other person sat in on the entire interview. The interview took between 20 and 40 minutes depending on the age of the interviewee.

Descriptive and inferential statistical analysis of the data was conducted primarily using the statistics package SPSS. A full explanation of the analytical strategies employed in the survey is provided in Eynon (2009). In summary, bivariate analysis, factor analysis, analysis of variance (ANOVA), and logistic and linear regression were utilised to explore the relationships between age, gender, attitudes, skills and contextual factors in understanding young people's uses of technology. A particular strength of the design of the survey is that we could make distinctions between the activities, attitudes, skills and contexts of a wide range of young people in the UK.

Unfortunately, we were unable to repeat the survey in the third year as originally intended, because one of the first actions taken by the new UK coalition government in 2010 was to close down a large number of its 'quangos' (organisations separate from but funded by central government), more or less starting with Becta. This affected the funding of activities such as the survey although we were still able to carry out the final year of interviews as originally planned. Thus we were able to observe the ways in which orientations towards technology seemed

to remain quite constant over time, while actual practices certainly did change, in response to a technology climate and market in a state of constant evolution or perhaps, as claimed by the industry at least, revolution.

Shape of the book

The aim of this book is to build up a fair and balanced picture of how digital technologies figure in the lives of teenagers presently. We are looking at teenagers in the technology-rich parts of the world, where the norm is to have access to a range of devices and the Internet, and we will not attempt to discuss those very many teenagers in parts of the world where there is little or no access to new technologies, nor in parts of the world where, although access is rapidly expanding, there is nonetheless very little socially-focused qualitative research available on what that means to them. But we are confident that many of the technology-related issues we discuss are recognisable in any society where young people are regularly using mobile phones, playing computer games, or accessing the Internet.

Within those acknowledged limitations, we attempt to address the broadest possible picture. We are not just interested in the vivid and extreme cases, and we do not buy the notion that young people, teenagers especially, are going somewhere that is beyond the understanding of the rest of us by virtue of their access to technologies. But it is by no means easy to judge whether or not the pervasive presence of digital technologies in young people's lives will turn out to have been a fundamental transformation in how they engage with the world, and with growing up, or something rather less momentous from a future perspective than many perceive it to be right now. The following two predictions, from a whole generation ago in fact, address a future that has now arrived and, although somewhat extreme, it would be hard to argue that the hopes and concerns expressed turn out to have been wholly unfounded, or reveal that we had in fact expected more than has been delivered by digital technology:

> The cumulative improvements in intellectual skills and creativity, coupled to a markedly expanded understanding of the world, will differentiate such children almost to the extent of forming a new species: *Homo sapiens cerberus* . . . [who] will survive, prosper, and in due course dominate all those who do not partake of the new intellectual technology.
>
> (Stonier and Conlin, 1985: 195–6)

> In the near future, all the representations that human beings have invented will be instantly accessible anywhere in the world on intimate, notebook-size computers . . . Instant access to the world's information will probably have an effect opposite to what is hoped: students will become numb instead of enlightened.
>
> (Kay, 1991: 138)

While the first of the above (despite the nonsense about a new species) raises a legitimate concern about inequity of access to the digital world, the second is concerned, with what many would consider equal legitimacy, about the intellectual welfare of those that gain such access. These turn out to be properly long-term concerns, and are at the heart of the various discussions that follow: in what ways, and from what perspectives, are teenagers experiencing new technologies in their lives, and how do sub-sections of that population vary from the mainstream experience?

Each chapter of the book addresses such questions, from a specific perspective. The following chapter, 'Uses', presents an overview of the things that teenagers who do have access to technologies actually do with them, and looks at how that breaks down within different sub-groups of the population in terms of intensity of engagement, orientation towards technology, and opportunity to use it. In Chapter 3: 'Contexts', we look at how technology is entering into, and possibly changing, the key contexts of teenagers' lives – home and school – and explore the question of whether, in fact, we might need to consider teenagers' digital worlds in their own right as a third key context of adolescence. Chapter 4: 'Identity' goes on to deal with one of the central perspectives on teenagers' digital lives, and explores the role played by networked technologies especially in processes of identity formation. Such processes can involve teenagers in the exploration of multiple aspects or versions of identity, and in this chapter we examine the ways in which online social contexts offer new kinds of opportunity for the exploration and presentation of identity.

In Chapter 5: 'Learning', we explore a topic that brings together many of the hopes and anxieties that both adults and teenagers have about digital technologies, which have accompanied the development of personal computing, and subsequently the Internet, from the earliest days. We explore the ways in which personal computers and the Internet have, or have not, succeeded in transforming formal education, and the ways in which teenagers experience new forms of learning in their various self-directed explorations of what technology has to offer. Chapter 6: 'Outliers', by contrast, confronts the somewhat less examined but equally

important issue of what happens to those teenagers who do not find themselves so well placed within the digital world, and who feel themselves to be deprived of opportunity, for self-improvement and for involvement in experiences that others in their peer group take for granted.

Finally, Chapter 7 engages with what we suggest is a markedly universal theme within adolescents' perspectives upon technology: the ways in which their access to the tools and networks of the digital world are particularly valued by teenagers for their capacity to enable and even speed up the acquisition of what lies at the heart of growing up: *autonomy*. Whatever their individual feelings about technology in certain respects, all teenagers appear to recognise it as instrumental in seeking independence in how they do the things they want and need to do throughout the phases of their adolescence, as their priorities shift from seeking the freedom to enjoy the things they want to enjoy, and establishing the social relationships they desire, towards beginning to take responsibility for their own futures in their studies and their thinking about employment possibilities.

The chapter, and the book, will end with some consideration of the 'futures' aspect of the various perspectives covered in the preceding chapters: the nature and relevance of their technology lives as teenagers moving into young adulthood, higher education and employment; the ways in which technologies and the ways young people use them continue to change and evolve; ending with some thoughts on the ways in which the concepts of teenager and technology might appear in a further generation's time.

2   Uses

There is a strong tendency, when discussing young people's relationship with new technology, to flourish lists of all the amazing things they do in the digital world:

> Computer games, email, the Internet, cell phones and instant messaging are integral parts of their lives.
>
> (Prensky, 2001)

> Our brains are under the influence of an ever-expanding world of new technology: multichannel television, video games, MP3 players, the Internet, wireless networks, Bluetooth links – the list goes on and on.
>
> (Greenfield, 2009)

> Social network sites, online games, video-sharing sites, and gadgets such as iPods and mobile phones are now well-established fixtures of youth culture.
>
> (Ito *et al.*, 2010: 1)

Whether enthusing (Prensky), sounding alarm (Greenfield), or developing a fresh discourse around the topic (Ito *et al.*), it is clearly hard to engage with the question of what it is that young people actually *do* with digital technologies without compiling lists. It is also our own experience, from our research in this field, that teenagers like to assemble and have available to them a collection of technology-powered activities of various kinds, from which they can choose in order to get jobs done, and keep themselves amused. In the course of this chapter, we present our own compilation of mainstream teenagers' technology practices, before going on to explore how their relationships to technology vary within that broad set of common activities.

The next section considers how those practices are formed and develop through the phases of childhood and adolescence, and summarises the repertoire of practices typically undertaken by mainstream teenagers. The following section, 'Variations around the mainstream', explores the considerable variation between teenagers in terms of attitudes towards technology, showing that the mainstream practices are only part of the picture. In 'Changes over time' we take note of the reality that teenagers' technology lives are in a state of constant flux, both in terms of what they do, and how they feel about those things.

Forming technology habits

As explained in the previous chapter, when we talk of new technologies we refer to two main perspectives: the different kinds of hardware that enable access to digital resources and networks, and the uses made of those resources and networks. In our research between 2008–2011, we asked young people to tell us about the wide range of such technologies they were using on a regular basis: desktop computers, laptops, phones, games consoles, and of course the Internet, as well as about the things they wished to use but could not, and the things they preferred not to use. As we shall see, the range of hardware available to them, and the ways in which they make use of this, were in a state of continuous evolution throughout that time, and continue to be so.

The conditions that enabled teenagers to collect together their wide array of digital activities can be located first in the explosion of hardware aimed in part at their age group – multiple types of games consoles, MP3 music players, teenager-oriented mobile phones – since the 1990s, and then in the rapid expansion of broadband connectivity in the UK throughout the first decade of the twenty-first century: by 2008, high speed Internet (almost exclusively via broadband) was available in the homes of something like 85 per cent of 12–15 year olds (Ofcom, 2010a). This represented a considerable change over the immediately preceding five years or so, as Livingstone's 2004 UK Children Go Online study indicates, when only 49 per cent of homes had access to the Internet overall, and while homes with young people in did have higher proportions of access (UKCGO reports 71 per cent of young people aged 9–19 having the Internet at home) this was mostly via dial-up, which did not allow for an Internet experience comparable to what was possible once broadband became available.

What struck us most forcibly from the start of our own study was the extent to which it appeared that the teenagers we spoke with were now making regular use of what is, to some considerable extent, a

common repertoire of digitally enabled activities. More important than the exact nature of specific activities and applications, perhaps, was the holistic nature of their digital lives: they tended to collect together and peruse their technology preferences like hobbyists, taking pleasure in the variety of choice at their disposal as much as in any one thing. This variety of technology possession and activity was gradually built up during the course of the pre-teen years, but most young people only seemed to achieve the full mainstream range around the beginning of the teenage years.

Phases of use

Steinberg divides adolescence into three broad phases: early adolescence, from about 10 to 13 years old; middle adolescence, from about 14 to 18 years, and late adolescence, which might then continue into the early 20s (2002: 4). At the same time, though, he points out that there is no way of agreeing clear boundaries for these phases, as they vary markedly according to different perspectives (e.g. biological, emotional, cognitive, social, educational etc.). In this book we loosely follow Steinberg's phases by referring to young people for the most part either as pre-teens, early teens, or mid-late teens.

The youngest children we spoke to – pre-teens – were already entering the final phase of primary school by the time we met them. In the case of these children, as they were in 2008, we saw a good range of technology explored, in fairly unstructured ways, by these 8 and 9 year olds. In many cases, it was evident that technology was generally not a first priority in their lives:

> maybe I would eat and then I might do either violin or play my steel pan and then I would go on the computer, my PSP or my PS2.
>
> (Dale, 9)

> I either chose a phone or a horse and I chose a horse because a phone was too much money . . . a horse is only about a hundred pounds and it can do anything you want it to do, but iPods is only like that big, but horses are like that big.
>
> (Vicki, 9)

Nonetheless, it did appear that this period of apprenticeship, in which access and scope of activity is likely to be far more constrained by parents than is the case when they become teenagers, is important in enabling these younger children to gradually gain some degree of control over,

and comprehension of, the digital world that is populated by their older siblings and their future selves:

> I'm only allowed [. . .] well I know the password for my normal proper email address but I'm not allowed to email anyone, only my mum and dad
>
> (Dale, 9)

> I'd like to . . . like use Internet chat rooms, my Mum wouldn't like let me.
>
> (John, 9)

In that context of generally quite close parental regulation at this age, many we spoke to were enthusiastically, if quite randomly, experimenting with different uses of the technology:

> normally I go on the Internet and play like Neopets or Sims, or I just go on Word and do my homework, or I do – got to Excel and do like times tables [. . .] and that's all I really do. [. . .] I've learnt how to put iTunes [. . .] and how to use Excel properly.
>
> (Ingrid, 9)

> Well I'm quite good at typing, I like just messing around, just going on all sorts of things, you know. [. . .] Well with the computer I know quite a lot and not much problems really come up usually.
>
> (John, 9)

> I like doing story . . . I like typing up stories on my computer and printing them out. And I like pretending that we're playing schools with my sister and pretending that a child made this and I have to read it.
>
> (Anne, 8)

The fairly random technology behaviours of this period start quite rapidly to conform to a shared pattern within the peer group as these young people approach and enter the teenage years. When we looked at what young people by the ages of 12–13 were telling us about the wide range of technology-enabled activities in their lives, it was possible to perceive a much more regular pattern of technology practices having already taken shape, even if we did not often find strong evidence of intensive engagement with any particular one of those practices. We most often heard about varieties of media consumption, in which uncomplicated

distraction provided by different forms of online entertainment was the norm more often than deep states of flow or single-minded engagement:

> It's more of like an accessory. So I'll be sitting in my room doing homework and always have my computer on because I will always be listening to music.
>
> (Emma, 15)

> I would hate it if I didn't have my Xbox, because it's just something to do if there's nothing, nothing else to do. It just like fills in any gaps sort of thing, so I probably wouldn't . . . I'd just die of boredom if I didn't have it, because it just fills in everything. Like in between like space if I'm like doing a bit of sport or something, to watch a show in an hour I'll just play it.
>
> (Dominic, 15)

The range of activities that constitutes the mainstream teenager digital technology use is characterized by interchangeability, rapid switching between activities rather than actual multi-tasking, and very often quite light involvement in a number of these activities: considerable variety spread thin, with certain (moderately stronger than the rest) preferences dominating, to some extent in line with the stereotype of girls favouring social networking –

> when I get home I normally go on my computer and chat to my friends, like on MSN and stuff like that. Sometimes I call them and I usually call them quite a lot and I go on my computer quite a lot as well, and texting and stuff like that . . . Quite a while. Um, like hours [laughs].
>
> (Zoe, 12)

– and boys of the same age favouring games-play, both online and offline:

> I've got like Gameboy, PSP, PS2, Nintendo Wii – [. . .] I use the Nintendo Wii quite a lot, because it's the new thing and it's got good graphics on it basically, and because I haven't got the PS2 working yet, because it's in a pile of junk somewhere . . .
>
> (Aaron, 13)

Within this mixed bag of communication and entertainment, we can also detect evidence of relatively constructive and creative activity being made possible, simply because the opportunity to do so is quite easily available:

I use Photoshop when I'm bored to just edit pictures and make them look funny.

(Babik, 13)

Making like loads of PowerPoint presentations and stuff about my life and what goes on, because I like doing that.

(Kathy, 12)

At the same time, the argument long deployed by young people to parents that computers and the Internet were vital to their studies appeared to be gaining traction as teachers in schools increasingly started to encourage their students to access the Internet at home for homework, or made use of virtual learning environments that could increasingly be reached from home. Having argued this partly because this gave them access to the other perceived benefits of computers, these teenagers did then find themselves very often using their new Internet-connected opportunities for schoolwork. Carrying out some degree of homework has indeed become a crucial item in the repertoire of online activities, whether simply because they have to fulfil the bargains they made with their parents or – and increasingly as they approach the age when the need for qualifications became more urgent – as a primary motivation for using technology at home. Thus, while the dividing line between using the computer for entertainment and using it for schoolwork is crossed all the time, it did appear that, for a great proportion of the young people we spoke to, study activities seemed to find a regular place in the wider array of home technology uses:

I go home and I go on my laptop and I often . . . it's more fun and stuff . . . you can play like sort of like activities and games and stuff but like you're learning at the same time. And it's like better . . . if you just sit there reading and it could be boring like.

(Emily, 14)

I'm doing my graphics coursework on it at the moment. And I listen to music, I go on YouTube, just because the bands I like are just so hard to find. So I do that and I email my friends.

(Debbie, 15)

I'm not trying to be buff or anything but I usually get on with my homework before I go on MSN, because if I'm on MSN I'll find someone decent to talk to and you talk for ages and by the times it's time to do my homework I'd just be like . . . ohh.

(Lucy, 13)

The shift towards a greater emphasis on using technology, and especially the Internet, to support schoolwork begins earlier for some than others, of course, but by the mid-teens it is more normal to encounter a greater prioritisation of schoolwork, and a proportionate reduction in other technology-related preoccupations. For many, this is already the case by the time they are 14 – around that time an increasing number begin to report growing dependence on Internet-connected computers for their studies:

> a lot of homework is research and you need to research on the computer. Because I don't mind using books but it's just available, readily available on the computer, so . . .
>
> (Matt, 15)

As the 2011 *EU Kids Online* study shows, study has become a core element of teenagers' online repertoire, with 85 per cent of 9–16 year olds across 25 European countries using the Internet for schoolwork, making it the leading single online activity carried out by teenagers. But enabling this move initiated what is in fact a quite radical change for young people: to be able to study, socialise and have fun on the same device. Whereas, previously, communication and entertainment technologies were very clearly demarcated from the serious business of schoolwork, there now appeared to be little way of distinguishing what children are exactly up to, onscreen. For young people and adults alike, this was proving to be both a positive and a negative (an issue we shall look at more closely in the next chapter), in that it did the good job of bringing young people into a zone of potential study whenever they sat down at their Internet-connected computer, but then this was also a study zone that constantly buzzes with all kinds of distraction.

Mainstream teenage technology uses

Thus, if we add in key activities such as online TV-on-demand viewing (just becoming established at the time our research began), mobile phone-enabled photography and movie making, and (more often than not at the time, illegal) music downloading, the mainstream teenage repertoire of technology use, as observed in our research, appeared to consist for the large proportion of young people of some combination of at least one instance (and possibly more) of each one of the following key categories:

- **social communication and networking:** via SNS (social networking sites); IM (Instant Messaging); texting; email;

- **consumption of entertainment media:** online and offline games play; music downloading and listening; watching TV on demand via the Internet; viewing video clips and movies online;
- **creative activities:** music composition and recording; video and photo creation and editing; composing stories, games; computerised artwork;
- **membership and participation:** via the Internet in offline and online groups and communities, for sport, affiliations (including school and college networks), online multiplayer games etc.;
- **school and college work:** production of work with office suite software; finding information using online search engines and encyclopedias; use of revision websites (e.g. BBC Bitesize); use of school Virtual Learning Environments and intranet.

Some items on this list have been familiar features of the teenage technology environment for many years previously, but it appears that – largely through the medium of their shared membership of peer group sub-culture – most had extended the scope of their activities to encompass this broader range of choice. Thus, it would be common to keep a number of options going throughout the evening – 'seven until I go to bed, I'm on the computer' (Leah, 13) – weaving a range of lines of alternative interest around that day's homework, touching on various elements within the general repertoire as they do so.

Variations around the mainstream

What is most striking about this generalised repertoire of teenagers' technology-based activities is the considerable variation among teenagers in terms of their feelings and attitudes regarding specific activities, and technology in general. We observed a spectrum of orientations, encompassing frustrated longing for technology among the dispossessed, mild approval for its utility from some mainstream teenagers, to quite generalised approval and satisfaction for all things technological among the majority of mainstream users, and much more sharply focused enthusiasm for specific and specialised uses of technology among a relatively small portion of the age group.

Table 2.1 provides a simplified representation of the overall adolescent population's engagement with technologies, both in terms of the phases of technology use through which they pass as they grow older, and the varying orientations towards it that take shape in their thinking and practices during that time:

Table 2.1 Representation of adolescent engagement with technologies

Pre-teenage	Early teenage	Mid-late teenage	Post-teenage
	Enthusiasts, intensive users	Enthusiasts, intensive and specialist users	
Apprentice-ship	Teenage mainstream users	Student mainstream users	Student/worker mainstream users
	Ambivalent users		
Intermittent users (unconnected and vulnerable)			

There are a number of quite important distinctions indicated here, between different kinds of young technology users. First of all, it is important to move beyond the popular perception that young people are, by definition, all out-and-out enthusiasts for technology, even if they are regular, mainstream users. Second, all generalisations about young people's uses of technology should recognise the (not sufficiently visible) fact that a number of young people have very limited access to technologies and the Internet in particular, apart from what is made available within formal education contexts (the central theme of Chapter 6). A European-wide survey in 2010 showed as many as 91 per cent of UK households with children having home Internet access, with a European average of 84 per cent (Eurostat, 2010). The strong UK figures reflected government efforts at that time to reduce Internet disadvantage among young people, in a programme that has since ended. (Whether 9, 16 or 50 per cent, depending on country, unable to connect to the Internet and therefore having to use school equipment, libraries, or friends' computers or devices, this represents significant numbers of children not being able to get on the Internet readily.)

Enthusiastic and intensive users

Thirdly, we need to pay close attention to the relatively small, but highly visible and (possibly) influential sub-group of enthusiasts and specialised users. These are the young people who have at times been taken to represent the whole age group, as 'net-gens' or 'digital natives', strongly devoted to using new technologies, exploring and extending the affordances of those technologies, trying out new devices whenever available, and spending a good deal of their time in complex acts of multitasking. While our attention throughout this book is to the wide teenage population, with its varying orientations towards technology, this group

merit considerable attention, if only for the way in which they embody so many assumptions about young people and technology within popular culture.

If digital natives do exist, it is only as a 'cultural subset of teens and young professionals', that have grown up 'immersed in the digital world where the Internet, personal computers, and modern technology are a commonplace convenience'.[1] The precise characteristics of what this subset is considered to be like tend to be redefined year-on-year, but usually involve elements such as a relaxed, problem-solving approach to making technologies work, a preference for (or addiction to, depending on your viewpoint) multi-tasking, a preference for information over hardware, and an open and unrestricted approach to collaboration, online and offline. Roughly 20 per cent of our sample (at most) appeared to correspond to this stereotype. These were the ones who appeared to be readily grasping and coping with the complexities of any new technology, making extensive use of online media for purposes of participation in different social groupings, producing as well as consuming online content, using the Internet wherever possible for academic study; constantly online and constantly multi-tasking.

When we started talking to the young people in our own sample, we were somewhat susceptible to the myth of the digital native as the teenage norm. Research does, after all, want to find out things that are interesting or remarkable, and qualitative research especially is sometimes susceptible to the allure of vivid findings. So, when we heard youngsters reporting in the following ways, it did momentarily at least seem that we finally had begun to find the kind of teenager that the popular media, and numerous online commentators, had led us to believe we would find in abundance:

> I do my homework on it, like research and everything like that. I talk to friends on it via MSN or Skype. I play games on it like World of Warcraft or Everquest 2 or something like that. Um, it's mainly just those. I go on YouTube and stuff like that and look at videos. I listen to music on it. It's my life bases around that really, I can't . . . because um I couldn't really live without the computer to be honest
>
> (Liam, 15)

> me and my friends we sort of dance, so we put some videos of us dancing . . . we were known, just in town, we're just walking around and, you guys are the ones.
>
> (Samuel, 15)

> I like to put photos on the Internet . . . I take my camera with me basically everywhere, so if I meet up with my friends on a Saturday we'll just take loads of photos and I'll put them up. And then people can look at them and they can comment on them and . . . yeah, and stuff like that. And I can edit them as well with some really basic Windows stuff where I can put it into black and white, or change the colour or get rid of red-eye. Which is quite useful because sometimes people will say, oh no my skin looks really blotchy and that, can you put it in black and white? So I do.
>
> (Debbie, 15)

These can all deservedly be viewed as strong examples of how youngsters can incorporate new technologies quite intensively and, in many ways, productively into their lives, and do so with a strong sense of their own agency (see Chapter 7). The first of these youngsters, Liam, went on to tell us how he had become addicted to playing World of Warcraft and then, with the help of his friends online, subsequently worked his way through and out of that. The broad picture of his technology use was, for all its significantly negative aspects at times, on balance an important and often positive aspect of his teenage years. The other two examples exemplify the ways in which digital technologies – including both technical tools such as cameras and photography software – can be combined with social networking resources to offer creative and socially active youngsters opportunities for learning, self-expression and active membership of a well-defined and responsive social network.

These teenagers were characterised by their *enthusiasm* for technology. They loved using technology, and given the opportunity, always chose the digital option:

> I get like virtually all of it from the web. My mum . . . went to the library and got some books on the Civil Rights Movement and I had a look through those. And I also had the Internet . . .
>
> (Trevor, 15)

Given a relentless hobbyist enthusiasm for pervasive digital technologies, it is hardly surprising that for such youngsters these technologies do indeed come to be the first choice for all the things they do, sometimes forming the backdrop to their lives, day and night:

> You don't have just a single track view, you don't have just the textbook . . . by accessing the Internet you get everyone's opinion from all over the world, whether it's right or wrong . . . yeah, all the

time. Especially helpful with homework. I think maybe ten years ago you'd phone a mate up and copy it down, but now – just on Facebook.

(Sean, 17)

My laptop stays on most of the night because if I have any ideas I'll be able to just get on there. [. . .] do a lot of writing until 2 o'clock in the morning and then I'll go, okay, leave it like that, go to bed and then at 4 o'clock in the morning I'll wake up, oh okay I have another idea, I'll get back on the computer again.

(Tom, 19)

The multi-tasking nature of these technology enthusiasts is central to this picture. Seen by some as evidence of how technology is helping them to engage in the modern world in a more creative manner and by others as evidence of diminished powers of concentration, our own research pointed us towards more than one way of thinking about multi-tasking. In our own nationally representative survey of young people aged 8, 12, 14 and 17–19 we found two distinct types of multi-tasking occurring, specifically while involved in homework: constructive multi-tasking (e.g. using a search engine; having instant messenger open; playing music) and distractive multi-tasking (e.g. using a computer to watch TV on demand; watching videos on a computer; playing games on a computer). These very different ways of combining technology activities were noted also in our qualitative studies, and indicated how some teenagers were actively creating digital environments that were conducive to study, while others were not (Eynon, 2009).

It is notable that as they entered mid-late teenager years, these young people appeared to be constructively multi-tasking to a greater extent than pre- or early teens. In Britain people from younger generations do appear in general to multi-task more than older generations (Helsper and Eynon, 2010). However, not much is actually known about when and how this can be a positive or negative aspect of young people's use of new technologies. Multi-tasking may have a negative impact on learning due to cognitive overload (Hembrooke and Gay, 2003), but the precise nature of the multi-tasking clearly needs to be considered.

The constructive aspect did indeed appear evident in some of our case study teenagers, when we visited them in their homes. Trevor, for instance, had established a typical repertoire of daily technology activities involving schoolwork, games playing, TV viewing on the computer and communicating with friends via Bebo and MSN Messenger, and typically can work with two distinct soundtracks in his head at one time: 'I prefer

playing games when I'm listening to music.' He also developed a strong interest in music technology, using quite sophisticated music composition software both for schoolwork and for fun:

> If I'm sitting at the PC, I'm usually just . . . the keyboard's on and I'm just playing something random with my left hand, and that's where my ideas come from, from me just randomly playing something and then I think 'That sounds quite nice, I could do –' so I go on, notate it and then I'll build on it with other instruments and stuff.
>
> (Trevor, 15)

The scope of such technological affordances that these particularly committed users discover for themselves is consistent with the observations arising from the three-year *Digital Youth Project* (Ito *et al.*, 2008, 2010), which provides a detailed analysis of the various levels and types of engagement with new technologies observed in American youth during that period. The authors of the report classified digital youth in terms of 'differing levels of investment in new media activities' in ways that reflect 'varying levels of technology- and media-related expertise, interest and motivation', for 'different youth at different times' (Ito *et al.*, 2010: 36). Three levels of engagement are named as 'hanging out', which is what the majority of youth are seen as doing via a range of communication media such as 'texting, instant messaging, mobile phones and Internet connections'; 'messing around', by which youth 'create and navigate new forms of expression and rules for social behavior', and 'geeking out', by which certain youths, within widely dispersed specialised social networks, 'dive into a topic or talent' via new media (Ito *et al.*, 2010: 1).

These are not seen as fixed categories of young people. The authors are above all concerned to present an account that recognises an 'overall constellation of characteristics . . . constantly under negotiation and flux as people experiment with new modes of communication and culture'. While we would question the claim that young people do in fact substantially change their fundamental relationship with technologies (our own evidence suggested that most adopt a particular orientation towards technology and do not move far from that over time), theirs is a valuably nuanced account of what young people do. Ito and colleagues make it clear that they are:

> wary of the claims that there is a digital generation that overthrows culture and knowledge as we know it . . . While the pace of

technological change may seem dizzying, the underlying practices of sociability, learning, play, and self-expression are undergoing a slower evolution, growing out of resilient social structural conditions and cultural categories that youth inhabit in diverse ways in their everyday lives.

(Ito *et al.*, 2010: 1)

Such a recognition is crucial to making sense of the relationship between technological change and people: changes in human behaviour are generally not uniform or unidirectional across any population. It certainly helps us to resist dazzling fantasies about wholesale generational change of the kind offered by people like Tapscott (1997 and 2009), which somewhat romantically presents a whole generation of young people as being transformed *en masse* by their immersion into digital practices. Referring back to his first book on the topic in the later publication, Tapscott goes so far as to claim that this 'unified' generation is changing the world, by 'using the Web and their social networks to discover and collaborate' (2009: 310).

He is by no means alone in asserting this order of generalisation. From a somewhat different starting point, the high profile British neuroscientist Susan Greenfield has on a number of occasions in recent years expressed views that strongly resonate with popular anxieties about the modern world, and modern youth:

Today's technology is already producing a marked shift in the way we think and behave, particularly among the young . . . We could be raising a hedonistic generation who live only in the thrill of the computer-generated moment, and are in distinct danger of detaching themselves from what the rest of us would consider the real world.

(Greenfield, 2009)

The problem lies not in the desire to make legitimate warnings, so much as the lack of direct evidence to support some of the claims made in support of them. Whether through Prensky's visionary perspective, with his faith in the capacity of digital natives to learn in radically new ways, or of Tapscott, with his faith in the new generation's wholesale rejection of the 'vile remnants of bygone days' (2009: 310), or Greenfield's warnings about the impact of technology over-use upon the capacity to form long-term human relationships (2009), the issue of what using technologies does to young people is one of those topics about which everyone perhaps has more opinion than information. All of them might be accused of two kinds of questionable assumption: first, that all

young people are intensive users of new technologies, and second, that those that do use them intensively are being substantively transformed by such experiences.

Equally misleading, we would suggest, is the popular belief that this group constitutes 'early adopters', pathfinders for practices that will eventually be common among all their peers. While they do demonstrate what might be achieved by certain kinds of young people who possess the resources and support networks to experiment and creatively develop creative uses of technology, there is no strong evidence to suggest that those practices will inevitably become the norm for the whole peer group.

More helpful perhaps is the attempt to conceptualise different patterns of use offered by Livingstone and Helsper in their four step 'ladder of opportunity' model (2007, focusing on children's Internet use), which observes that as children become older and more experienced with the Internet they are more likely to undertake a wider range of online activities. In this model, younger children and new users of the Internet tend first to undertake information seeking then, as they become more experienced, go on to play games and use email. As children gain experience in using the Internet they take up a wider range of activities that involve peer to peer engagement, such as instant messaging and downloading music. The fourth step on the ladder encompasses an even wider range of activities such as contributing to discussion forums or signing petitions and this stage is seen in teenager users who are very frequent (daily) users of the Internet. Not all young people reach the later stages, and may need support to get there (Livingstone and Helsper, 2007). While initially this ladder of opportunity was first identified in empirical research in the UK, it was later shown to apply across Europe (Livingstone *et al.*, 2011).

Thus, while through studying the sub-group of enthusiasts and specialist users we can perhaps encounter interesting and innovative possibilities in their uses of technologies, there is just as much to be learnt from what the less obviously remarkable users choose to do, or not to do, in their technology lives. This is especially so with respect to the shifting fashions and preferences that characterise the constantly changing picture of technology use in the age group.

Changes over time

In the final year of our research, we detected some evidence that a number of young people who engaged in the typical range of main-stream technology practices were becoming more ambivalent about

doing so than they had seemed when we first spoke to them three years previously. It seemed to be the case that for a number of young people, early tentative engagement does not necessarily flower into full-scale enthusiasm, and finally in this chapter we consider some possible reasons for this, in the context of considering changes that have taken place during the years following our initial interviews.

While superficially the ways in which people have come to use new technologies do not appear to change a great deal from year to year, we are constantly being promised stunning new benefits by the technology market, and at the same time we share in a global process of appropriation of those technologies, which very often subverts the intentions of the designers and manufacturers. Some would claim, such as during the time of the riots in the UK in the summer of 2011, when smartphones were blamed for enabling sudden mass gatherings of uncontrolled young people, or during the Arab spring earlier that year, that such processes were taking the digital dream in quite unexpected directions. Manuel Castells for example, ended a talk later in 2011[2] with the words 'now is the time to panic', suggesting that we are only now arriving at the start of the real impact on society of the digital revolution, and an impact that was brought about by the way people used those technologies, rather than by the technologies themselves.

It is hardly surprising then that teenagers do not show much sign of settling down to a steady state of technology use. They might well be doing broadly the same sorts of things in 2011 that they were doing in 2008 and, in many respects, in 2005, 2000 or even earlier: talking to friends old and new, joining social networks, playing games, studying, downloading stuff, browsing, shopping, wasting time and having fun. But the detail of what these things are, the ways in which they are connected, selected, strategised, monetised, and integrated into young people's lives never settle down to a steady state. There are too many drivers behind these habits to make it possible to predict which direction young people, as a socio-cultural entity and as a target market, will take, and it is even far from easy to know what happened retrospectively.

What we can say with some certainty is that by late 2009, Facebook had become the dominant focus of most young people's online lives in the UK, and in many other (but not all) parts of the world. For the younger UK teenagers, Bebo had until then been the preferred social network (where previously it had been MySpace), but when the younger teenagers who used it discovered they could join Facebook, most acted decisively and ruthlessly – 'I closed it. October I think' (Fiona, 14) – bringing it to the edge of collapse faster than could ever have been anticipated. While

not every one of them bought into the Facebook migration ('I'm just about the only person who doesn't!' explained 15-year-old David), it soon became the default for social engagement which required a conscious choice of self-exclusion or, by contrast, a considerable desire for self-inclusion on the part of those without home access to the Internet.

The quite complex issue of teenagers' experience of Facebook will be explored in greater depth in Chapter 4, but here we simply signal this notable example of how rapidly change in young people's technology habits can occur:

> the one word that springs to mind is Facebook. Massive part of my technology.
>
> (Fiona, 14)

For the UK teenagers, the hours of the evening after their tea, during homework and beyond, are generally now conducted within the connectedness of this nearly all-embracing network:

> Listen to my iPod on the way home, text friends cos you're not with them anymore, um use the computer to like talk to them on Facebook and stuff like that.
>
> (Fiona, 14)

As we said, not everyone uses it all the time, or unreservedly enjoys it, but few find it possible to conduct the business of being a teenager without it:

> I check – not very often . . . just to see any notifications . . . just like, people's birthdays, whether anyone's sent you any messages regarding school or sports or anything . . . or one of my friends would say what was the homework or something and I'd be able to answer that.
>
> (Joseph, 15)

Aiming to provide routes into the whole of its users' online lives – game play, video-viewing, affiliations with a range of groups, the opportunity to participate in major waves of social and political change – in some respects the scope of Facebook's potential reach is currently (2012) still immense. But it is also likely to be the case that Facebook's long-term ambitions must also contend with an inevitable stage of fatigue or even revulsion on the part of many users. While it is indeed clearly a massive

presence in very many young people's lives, we also found evidence that it carried some responsibility for the aforementioned change that we observed over the last three years: the slight but distinct cooling down on the part of some young people towards aspects of life online, such as the negative aspects of how Facebook is used within the peer group, or the negative attitudes towards it from both parents and teachers, as something that runs counter to educational success.

We would not wish though to confuse this ambivalence with hostility: out and out rejection of digital technologies by members of the age group is rare, and negative feelings about them tend to be complex and contradictory, relating more often than not to the frustrations of exclusion in a world of activity where every other young person seems to be included: 'I don't use them often – don't have a computer – nothing nothing nothing nothing all blocked – I would like a computer at home and Internet and I would like a phone that actually works' (Tim, 14). In the light of such frustration, the problem of trying to exercise self-control over the use of technologies that enable most teenagers to manage their own explorations of friendship, knowledge and possibilities for their own future seems, by comparison, to be worth grappling with – as this selection of comments from 16-year-old Jasmine demonstrate:

> I am very easily distracted if I am on a computer . . . So I try to stay away from it with work . . .
>
> I'll just type in whatever question's on my mind because, you know, you can put your Facebook status and ALL your friends will see that . . .
>
> I'm interested in going into medicine. So I – any university that has put up their stuff [on iTunes U], I'll just download ALL of them and listen to the ones that I'm interested in.

Summary

In this chapter we have tried to present a case that might at first seem to contradict itself, in both building a picture of what the mainstream of teenagers typically tend to do with the technologies in their lives, and then saying that actually this mainstream is not the whole picture. The point is, though, that the pattern of uses we identify is indeed shared by nearly all teenage technology users (and desired by those excluded from such use), but that does not mean that all of them feel the same way about those things: some develop intensive interests in technology that appear excessive to their peers, while others want to keep what they see as the uncritical enthusiasm of mainstreamers at arm's length.

But neither should we make too much out of the notion that young people are turning away from digital technologies, as a consequence of overload and excessive access. This is clearly not the case, but equally the picture is far more complex than the likes of Prensky predicted ten years ago:

> A really big discontinuity has taken place. One might even call it a 'singularity' – an event which changes things so fundamentally that there is absolutely no going back. This so-called 'singularity' is the arrival and rapid dissemination of digital technology in the last decades of the 20th century.
>
> (Prensky, 2001: 1)

Technologies change faster than people, and people respond by adapting them to their own needs and choices on their own terms. For the most part, young people consume the popular media placed before them, gladly incorporating them into their lives, and looking for ways in which they benefit from them, as the following statistics from Ofcom indicate:

> scheduled television viewing on a television set, which attracted a daily reach of 72%. Text communication was primarily texting, which was done by 43% of the sample, and social networking on a computer, which was done by 40% on a daily basis. Playing games on a TV console attracted a higher daily reach among boys (46%) than girls (10%).
>
> The key media devices for 12–15 year olds were the TV and the computer. Seventy-five per cent of the time that 12–15 year olds spent on media and communications activity was spent using a TV or a computer. The mobile phone accounted for a further 10% of media time.
>
> The Internet was an integral part of most 12–15 year olds' lives. 12–15 year olds almost universally saw it as a useful source of information and it was widely used for fun and for contact with other people. In addition to the core activities of social networking and emailing, it was used for finding information for school or homework or on subjects of personal interest.
>
> (Ofcom 2010b)

Young people view and use technologies as individuals growing up within the social and cultural world of adults, and as actors within a

teenage culture that is strongly characterised now by the use of certain digital tools. In this book we are interested especially in the ways in which the experience of being a teenager shapes, and is shaped by, their engagement collectively and as individuals with digital technologies. This is the case whether they are enthusiasts, positive users or those less convinced, or would-be users, frustrated by their lack of opportunity and dreaming of the great things they would do if they could try these things out for themselves.

3   Contexts

All you need is a screwdriver and an empty house.

Andrzej, Polish language student and
self-taught IT enthusiast

Has free access to the universe of the Internet, via more digital devices than any parent can keep track of, really enabled young people to create for themselves worlds that are new and unknowable (to adults) within the core contexts of their adolescence? Some would argue that access to digital technologies is enabling young people to alter their worlds in quite substantial ways:

> . . . children are using new technologies and digital media to build social connections across space-time, produce virtual 'places' in online spaces, and otherwise interrupt the spatiotemporal contours of their lives.
>
> (Leander *et al.*, 2010: 330)

There is a hint of Midwich Cuckoos in the idea of young people systematically re-engineering the spatiotemporal contours of their lives, which presumably are mainly found in the physical and cultural settings of home and school. Such anxieties are not without foundation, on the evidence of recent years of Facebook, BBM (Blackberry Messenger, low cost texting), World of Warcraft, MSN, but there is little new about the idea of teenagers ignoring the walls that adults place around them (cf. Shakespeare, W. *Romeo and Juliet*[3]).

The question we explore in this chapter is whether or not the apparent freedom to participate in their own online social networks – which some would argue constitute an alternative context of adolescence in their own right – is substantively altering teenagers' relationship to the traditional

contexts of their adolescent years, exposing them to different kinds of developmental opportunities, or risks. In the chapter that follows, we first of all discuss, in the sections on 'Home' and 'School', how the traditional contexts of teenagers' lives are both shaped in new ways by the arrival of digital technologies, and also how those contexts shape the ways that these technologies are used. Then in 'New worlds, old worlds' we consider whether the expansion of teenagers' technology lives in fact constitutes the formation of a brand new context of adolescence in its own right.

Home

We have learnt to think of the home as a highly enclosed and protective environment, but we should remember that current high levels of protectiveness towards adolescents is a relatively recent and – globally speaking – localised phenomenon, limited to the more privileged socio-economic groups around the world which prefer and are able to keep their teenage children within the boundaries of home and school during adolescence, rather than sending them out to contribute to the family income.

During the twentieth century, according to Crockett (1997), childhood became sentimentalised to the extent that using children for economic gain came to be seen as emotionally suspect, especially within middle-class families in the developed world, so that 'Children and young adolescents were recast as emotionally priceless but economically useless' (1997: 30). Changes in the labour market also contributed to a widespread shift in the major sphere of activity for adolescents from the workplace to educational settings, which had multiple implications for the experience of teenagers: they have become increasingly segregated from the adult world, and experience greater restrictions in terms of access to the hazards of street life (Zelizer, 1985 cited in Crockett, 1997: 30), their status within the family has become less autonomous and more dependent, and the period of adolescence has extended in order to accommodate increased demand for education and training in order to gain employment in the growing service sector (ibid.: 31). Crockett goes on to suggest that these changes have had negative impacts upon adolescents' psychological wellbeing, in terms of a sense of alienation from the adult world and an inclination towards certain symbols of adulthood such as material goods, alcohol use and sex (ibid.: 32).

Such an analysis, while clearly reflecting an increasingly common reality within the developed world, and some parts also of the developing world, does perhaps suggest that that very prosperity might lead to high

degrees of frustration and potential conflict for teenagers. Smetana, though, in a more recent analysis (2011), argues that 'intense and angry conflict with parents is not the norm' for many adolescents nowadays:

> despite persistent mentioning of a 'generation gap' or youthful rebellion, the evidence suggests that teenagers do not rebel against their parents, nor do adolescents reject all parental values. Adolescents look to their parents for advice, typically hold similar values to those of their parents on political, social and religious issues, and report that they admire their parents.
>
> (2011: 30)

At the same time, the present era of highly engaged and concerned parents, whose anxieties about the modern world are exacerbated by, and often tend to focus in particular upon, fears about technology, does in some cases result in considerable pressure on many young people. Smetana refers to the emergence of the 'helicopter parent', whereby particularly close attention is paid to academic success, and the avoidance of negative experiences. Such parents 'do not let their children grow up and handle difficult experiences on their own. Instead, [they] inappropriately continue to manage their children's lives right through college' (Smetana, 2011: 6). Even if parents are not excessively shadowing their children's every move, many teenagers themselves are only too aware of the dangers of leaving education without the qualifications they have been told will secure their futures.

Given the fact that the home within the developed world is at least as important as the school in terms of providing access to the digital domain, the pressure on parents to provide and accommodate Internet-connected computers for their children by the time they hit adolescence has grown almost irresistible. Ba *et al.* (2002) claim that the development of children's computing practices are most influenced by the home context through factors such as 'length of time children had a computer at home, a family's ability to purchase stable Internet connectivity; the number of computers in the home and where they are located; parents' attitudes toward computer use; children's leisure time at home; the computing habits of children's peers; and the technical expertise of friends, relatives and neighbours' (ibid.: 13 and 33). A few years on, in 2008 (by which time stable Internet access had become more normal), our own findings reflected these conclusions very closely: the home environment, and parents within that, seemed to us to be the key factor out of all, including the school, in how young people learn to use, and form their personal orientations towards, digital technologies.

Parental strategies for dealing with the opportunities and problems raised by such provision vary considerably, and in one way or another are always a significant factor in how adolescents themselves come to use technology in the long term. For many youngsters the ways in which their parents articulate and operationalise their feelings about how they should and should not use technology turns out to be perhaps the most significant factor of all. This can be seen as being the case whether they are strong in support, indifferent, or highly resistant – although in fact it is most usual to encounter some degree of combination of all three orientations.

The material presence of technology in the home

Despite their anxieties, parents buy or make available computers for their children, ostensibly for the purpose of supporting their learning, but more profoundly because there is felt to be some kind of underlying imperative to do so:

> I think it wouldn't be fair on him for his future to deny him the right to get the exposure of a computer [. . .] the more skill he has, the more he understands how people use them you know, it just gives him a better chance in life with jobs and you know his work future and studies.
>
> (parents of Adam, 9)

All the parents we spoke to had made sure that their children had fair to good access to computers and the Internet, often with more than one machine to choose from. So, in one family one would find that the father had his own computer, to which access was rare in order to ensure that none of his work was deleted, and the children had a desktop dedicated to their own uses, and a further laptop if the 'children's computer' was occupied. In another family, the teenager shared a computer with the rest of his family, located in his brother's bedroom on the ground floor, which all the family could use when necessary (with another computer upstairs without connections to the Internet or a printer, so not often used). This family operated a co-operative form of sharing: 'Whoever's got the most important job, they get it [to use the computer], so if a person is playing games and somebody else needs to do their homework then the person who needs to homework will get it.'

Another family had recently moved the computer to a spare room upstairs, having originally thought it was safer (when children were younger) to keep the computer within sight downstairs so they could

monitor it – 'you've got to know what your children are up to so that if
they're up to no good, you know they are up to no good!' – but eventually
that came to be distracting, as there was not a lot of space downstairs
and the TV was on while the teenage daughter was doing homework.

Access often involved quite complicated arrangements within houses
that mostly do not possess convenient spaces for machines, so that very
often children find themselves working with computers in hallways, on
landings, or on moveable trolleys. The main computer in 15-year-old
Trevor's house, for instance, lived on the dining-room table, and had to
be removed when guests came. The shift to laptops has gradually offered
greater flexibility, but the presence of these in shared living spaces still
can cause problems. Quite often teenagers preferred to work with a laptop
on their knees while sitting on a soft chair or sofa, and this in turn would
cause tensions in the way it indicated to some parents an insufficiently
serious orientation towards schoolwork:

> that really irritates me. He doesn't sit at a table or a desk, and he
> will often try and do several things at once. So he will have an MSN
> conversation going while he's got his maths homework on his lap
> and that really irritates me. We have a number of battles over that.
>
> (mother of Trevor)

She had ensured from the start of the family's technology history that
computers were always placed where their use could be viewed easily,
and as a single parent she felt that she had a major responsibility to
participate actively in her children's learning. In this household, the
computer constituted the nexus of a wide range of core family activities:
it both represented a potential danger in the eyes of Trevor's mother (in
terms of distraction and risk), and a powerful learning, as well as social,
medium round which the whole family might gather on occasions.

These makeshift arrangements reflect the somewhat salient fact that
computer and peripheral hardware – large and noisy desktop machines,
cathode ray tube monitors, printers, servers, games machines and of
course endless cables – proved hard to accommodate within homes,
during the quite long initial years of integration into the home. Indeed,
the inconvenience they undoubtedly caused within many homes
demonstrates the lengths that families will go to in order to support their
children's perceived right to learn how to use a computer. Eventually,
without doubt, the computer will transform into something that is
incorporated easily in the home, and the early days of incongruous office
machines sitting incongruously in living space will look quite quaint. It
is happening already in the form of slim laptops, iPads, multipurpose

giant TV screens, and other actual or potential solutions to accessing the Internet, digital communication media, and games wherever and whenever we want in the home: what we can be absolutely sure of is that as time goes by, we will notice these things less, while having them more and more present in our lives.

Managing the use of technology in the home

Livingstone and Helsper identified certain patterns in the ways that parents have dealt with the presence of new media in the home, back to the time before the Internet had become the dominant source of concern for many parents:

> parents seem engaged in a constant battle with their children as they seek to balance the educational and social advantages of media use and the negative effects that some content or mediated contact might have on children's attitudes, behaviour, or safety.
>
> (2008: 581)

These authors (referring especially to Nathanson, 1999, 2001) outline three broad strategies of parental regulation, namely active, restrictive, and co-viewing mediation (ibid.: 583), which they suggest has subsequently come to be applied by parents to the regulation of Internet use of their children:

> Parents have a preference for social over technical forms of mediation, preferring active co-use over technical restrictions, interaction restrictions, and monitoring practices.
>
> (ibid.: 596)

As was explained in a previous paper (Davies, 2011), the findings from our research identified something of this range, though more often than not with parents moving between one strategy and another, from laissez-faire to co-use or restrictive regulation, until such times as something goes markedly wrong. Whatever their approach, though, many parents increasingly perceive the Internet, whether used for schoolwork, socialising or leisure activities (in the perception of many parents, often all at once), as a significant focus for their concerns about many issues relating to their children's journey from childhood towards independence, including educational progress, social behaviour and risk. Equally, very many others do not regulate technology and Internet use very much, although these tend to be less vocal about their lack of concern than are

the anxious ones: first because lack of concern is not a particularly evangelical position to hold, and second because anything suggestive of a *laissez faire* attitude to children's safety is quite difficult to argue currently.

In a focus group discussion we held with a small group of parents in one school, the discussion came down to a stand-off between one strongly technology-resistant mother – 'I'm just so anti-it' – and a father who was both accepting of and positive about his 9-year-old son and 12-year-old daughter's uses of technology gaming, finding that it brought them closer together and is a social activity. This father felt that his children had learnt from their discussions with one another and reading instructions onscreen, and went so far as to suggest that having an interest or obsession with something can be healthy – 'I just think it's quite natural'. In reply the mothers present generally felt that they have negative experiences with gaming, such as children being in a bad mood when coming off the machine, or not knowing what else they can do if they are not allowed on the computer.

Parental anxieties are understandably higher regarding younger children, but the impact of excessive concern on some children is likely to be lasting, especially on those children who, as Smetana suggests, buy into their parents' values more generally. The 9-year-old boy who says 'I get stomach ache from guilt if I do anything on my mum's computer without telling her' (Peter) is potentially developing quite ambivalent views towards technology which, in the case of a number of young people we talked with, can quite easily remain with them into adolescence. We found plenty of instances in our research that suggest that the ways in which young people come to shape their own uses of technology reflect above all what parents do, and do not do, in terms of supporting, regulating and attempting to steer their technology uses. The history of each family's engagement with technologies reflects core family values, and is marked by shared achievements and sometimes crises that have come to crystallise that family's particular technology narrative. Although the range of issues confronted within families is fairly consistent across households – coping with the costs of equipment, deciding where to place it, learning how to make it work, trying to ensure that it enhances rather than hinders learning, balancing aspirations about long-term benefits with anxieties about present dangers, setting boundaries regarding its use – the ways in which these are confronted or resolved vary considerably from home to home.

These values relate closely to what Silverstone *et al.* refer to as the moral economy of the household, whereby all the objects of the household have particular meaning with regard to 'household practices and relations'

(1992: 15ff). This is especially the case with media objects – televisions, and personal computers – which have the role of bringing meanings from the public sphere into the private, enabling the 'crucial work of social reproduction'. They recognise that new media 'pose a whole set of control problems for the household, problems of regulation and of boundary maintenance' (1992: 20), and explore (tentatively but accurately as it has turned out) how the personal computer might constitute a similar threat, in terms of transgressing the boundaries round the home.

They also note that 'different families will draw on different cultural resources, based on religious beliefs, personal biography, or the culture of a network of family and friends, and as a result construct a . . . bounded environment – the home' (1992: 19). In our research, we met families who have rejected the television (for reasons related to their religious beliefs that lead them to resist what they see as the relentless flow of undesirable content from the public world into the private) and, while willing to use the Internet for accessing content from the public world, were not entirely happy about doing so. One family shared the belief that the use of mobile phones is 'rubbish. Totally irrelevant to anybody's living and just costing a lot of money'.

> we do not think it is all that worthwhile to stare into this box all the time. And we all feel, including the children, that we wouldn't know when to watch the telly really, we keep ourselves busy otherwise.
> (mother of Francesca, 13)

Francesca said that she was keen not to waste her time on the Internet, and her social networking was limited to participating in a religious discussion forum. While she did sometimes play games in school, at the end of lessons if the opportunity arose, she stated that she felt she should be using the Internet less than she did. Similarly, 15-year-old Jenny did use Facebook quite regularly in order to keep in touch with friends in other countries, and especially those from her religious community, while being conscious of not sharing the musical interest of her peers, her own being exclusively Christian rock music. For such families, it did seem that a real tension existed with respect to benefiting from being able to access knowledge, education and even entertainment from the outside world (Jenny's family indulged in the once weekly iPlayer access to popular documentaries), without succumbing to what they perceived to be negative and anti-social distractions from the TV screen and, quite often also, the Internet.

In different ways, teenagers also learnt to manage sometimes inconsistent moral economies when necessary, such as when they effectively

lived multiple technology lives by virtue of their parents having separated, each establishing within their new homes a distinctive media ideology (sometimes in striking contrast to one another). The mother of one girl, Anna, already concerned about the fact that her daughter had previously come across unacceptable content on the Internet, and might also have given away information about herself on social networking sites, had taken quite strict measures within her home. She aimed to exercise total control, at least when Anna was in her home, to the extent that she only allowed her onto the Internet via a laptop that was in the kitchen when she was able to oversee her. She also admits to regularly checking her daughter's website history and her contacts list on MSN. These measures also included a blanket ban on viewing YouTube unsupervised, and so was consequently very shocked to discover from Anna that she was free to do so when staying in her father's house. In effect, separated parents often seem to provide quite distinctive moral economies with specific regards towards the technology and Internet use they enabled or permitted in their particular home, which their children learn to move between with varying degrees of ease.

The extent to which, and manner in which, parental concerns impacted upon teenagers' behaviour in fact varied very considerably, with quite subtle differences from one household to the next. In the case of some intensive users, it was evident that parental reservations and regulation about computer use had a marked effect on what they revealed about their online behaviours, but not on the behaviours themselves:

> I might write myself a little task sheet or action plan or something, you need to get this done by this day. I've got coursework dates and all sorts of things so I just plan around my days. Cos the thing is I may get all of the work done now so I have maybe a day free, and that day when I'm sitting here I've got everything done and I can relax, that day, that's when she comes and says why aren't you revising?
>
> (Samuel, 15)

> they know I go on like MSN and that but they don't think I go on MSN while I'm doing the work. *[So you have to keep it hidden?]* Yes.
>
> (Nigel, 15)

Others, though, have quite readily and willingly internalised their parents' values and concerns about computer use:

[Do you have rules in the family for how much time you're allowed to spend?] Um not like definitive, but if I get told to come off I usually come of . . . if I get told to go do something . . . yeah. You must always prioritise. That's just something that goes on in the background in a way.

(Francesca, 14)

I am very easily distracted if I am on a computer . . . So I try to stay away from it with work . . .

(Jasmine, 16)

There are also plenty of young people who live in households where technology is central to the family economy (one or both parents substantially working with and in IT), for whom the home experience of using technology is both rich and approved. Tom, 19, for instance lived in a home with a sophisticated home network set up by his father, where each member of the family (father, mother, brother and Tom) had their own private technology setup in their own room. This formed the starting point of a technology-based trajectory through his education and on into employment in the future:

It's always been technology. Technology since I was . . . since as far as I can remember I've always been into technology. I've always loved different kind of equipment. I started my whole music production like when I was 12 when I first got my first computer.

These are merely the complex and interesting variations on the kinds of shared technology world found within the great majority of homes in a relatively developed and prosperous technology-rich society such as the UK. Certain battles are fought – won, lost or ending in compromise – over how the family as a whole permits and enables its members to use technology when at home. These variations are very important in the lives of young people, but only constitute one dimension of where and how teenagers' online lives are carried out.

School

Opportunities to continue out-of-school uses of technology when in school have been limited or non-existent until quite recently for most young people. If we are to believe claims such as the following, the value of teenagers' technology activities outside school – 'instant messaging, blogging, sharing files, consuming and producing media, engaging in

affinity spaces, gaming, building social networks, downloading answers to homework, and researching for school projects and assignments' – is markedly greater, 'more goal-driven, complex, sophisticated, and engaged' (Steinkuehler, 2008: 3), than anything that goes on in school.

Until recently at least, it is indeed the case that most children experienced minimal opportunity within school to use technology on their own terms. Personal devices have been banned either from school or, at least, from classrooms, games consoles were not been permitted, and casual or personal use of Internet-connected computers within school is mostly rendered fairly pointless by high levels of filtering ('Everything is blocked'; 'Don't be so petty by blocking websites like games'; 'I wish we could text each other, listen to music and be able to use MSN etc. in breaks'). Despite generally low approval for ICT lessons aimed at teaching teenagers how to use technology (see Chapter 5 also), most efforts to use technology within the wider curriculum were reported in positive terms in our own study, either because they offer a well-focused and stimulating experience of technology enhanced learning – students frequently report high satisfaction when ICT is used by thoughtful and innovative teachers – or because they simply provide an opportunity for young people to do their own thing for a while. But such technology usage still varies markedly even with schools with strong reputations for using technology within some subjects, reflecting both a lack of confidence on the part of many teachers, and insufficient resources to enable regular or spontaneous use across the curriculum.

But there are signs now that this picture is beginning to change. With respect to insufficient technology resources, we are witnessing the beginnings of some willingness to think what was previously considered unthinkable, and allow the teenagers themselves to provide part of the solution. In the United States, some high schools operate bring-your-own-device (BYOD) policies which, according to one teacher, have introduced a whole new dimension of connectivity and engagement for her students in their learning, such as when the school network went down one afternoon:

> In the past, this would have ended the activity right then and there. But this time, it wasn't a problem. Many students simply pulled out their own smartphones and went to work. Those without phones teamed up with their neighbors. By the end of the period, all 27 students were working on their assignments collaboratively on personal devices. And they had done exactly what we educators always dream of: They assessed their learning needs and found the right tools to satisfy those needs without adult intervention.
>
> (LaMaster and Stager, 2012: n.p.)

Such policies are likely to become increasingly common, if only for the two central reasons that students bring their own devices with them anyway, and this offers an economically attractive solution to the problem of providing universal access to the Internet within school. Other arguments include the need to leverage the flexibility of cloud computing, and a means of fostering self-directed learning. At the same time, many professionals perceive serious problems relating to equity and student online safety, and are dubious about the usefulness of smartphones for educational purposes beyond downloading information. But it does appear that resistance is thawing: one American high school's BYOD policy is notably simple and brief, permitting students' own devices on condition that doing so:

- imposes no tangible cost to the District;
- does not unduly burden the District's computer or network resources;
- has no adverse effect on . . . a student's academic performance.[4]

This sounds, and probably is, a very positive step in many respects. But there is no escaping the change represented here in terms of school opening the doors to young people being able to use their own devices as they choose, and thus rapidly becoming one more location where students can engage in digital communications and social networking with relative freedom. We explored these questions in a secondary school in the south of England very recently, and found that there was both quite high smart-phone ownership even among these 12–13 year olds – four had no mobile phone, ten had ordinary mobile phones, and ten had smartphones, even at this age. We discussed what they used their phones for, and the class's teacher joined in the discussion, to ask his class to tell him honestly whether anyone had *ever* engaged in a Facebook conversation during one of his lessons. Well over half the class cheerfully put up their hands.

Couple this with the incessant low-level chatter of BBM throughout the school day, and the suspicion begins to dawn that teenagers might be animating and populating a separate universe of their own right within the bounded and codified world of formal classrooms as well as within the private and secure space of the home; a rising wave of teenage activity that has been growing stronger and bigger for some time, largely unseen and unheard, right in front of the grown-ups.

Choosing and using digital media in school

Clearly many youngsters are in a position now to choose between a range of digital communication modes, and to use these more or

less whenever and wherever they like, including in school. Sonia Livingstone suggests that:

> young people evaluate the available forms of communication according to their distinct communication needs, making careful choices among face-to-face, writing, email, instant message, chat rooms, telephone, social networking, text messaging and so forth, and treating face-to-face conversation as one form among many.
>
> (Livingstone, 2009: 98)

Out of the class of 24 teenagers mentioned in the previous section, there certainly were a number of youngsters of this kind, choosing freely between a number of possible communicative choices: such as the one who said she used BBM 'all day', and both MSN and Facebook (which she accessed by smartphone) on an 'hourish' basis, doing so at 'home or anywhere to be honest!' (meaning, with a certain delicacy, school). A few others told us they favoured combinations such as Facebook, MSN, text and email (calling into question the accepted wisdom that digital youth spurn that last form of communication), with the addition in one case of LiveProfile (an app for the HTC smartphone) *and* phonecalls (fairly atypical). The majority, though, reported mainly using just two forms of communication: which is to say, in nearly every case, Facebook plus one: either texting or MSN. A very few used even less – just email, or just texting, or nothing at all – and even within the Facebook majority there were wide divergences of commitment or enthusiasm, reflecting the range of engagement with technologies outlined in the previous chapter: enthusiast, teenage mainstream, ambivalent.

At this age, on the contrary, it appears that the majority – that is, all with the exception of the enthusiasts, who love to explore new forms of digital communication whenever they get the chance – choose a particular kind of digital communication for what are mainly quite practical reasons in ways that supporters of uses and gratifications theory would suggest (LaRose *et al.*, 2001): because it is free or very low cost; because it fits in well with other activities they are doing at the time; because their immediate peer group favour it; because their parents allow them to use it; because (a fairly recent criterion) it is usable in school. There is nothing new about teenagers operating their own channels of communication throughout the school day, either blatantly or secretly, while the dominant discourses of school carry on in front of them.

Digital media have of course enabled a very much greater flow of information than used to be possible and, to varying extents, a greater range of choices that teenagers can make in order to nurture and pursue

their ongoing social interaction. In her book on how young adults use different kinds of digital communications for breaking up with partners, Ilana Gershon deploys the notion of *media ideologies*, 'beliefs about how a medium communicates and structures communication' (Gershon, 2010: 18). Media ideologies, she explains, are responsible for corollary information that is communicated alongside a particular message, within a particular form of communication: 'One never sends a message without the message being accompanied by second-order information; that is, without indications about how the sender would like the message to be received' (ibid.: 18). So in the case of her study, one young woman felt that her boyfriend had violated a tacit assumption about communication by texting her with the news that he was breaking up with her, when she felt that everyone knew that texting was appropriate only for light-hearted conversations (ibid.: 20). Gershon's argument is that these media ideologies are neither true nor false in themselves, but are simply beliefs that influence how people communicate, and make sense of the communications of others.

Teenagers clearly do hold some explicit beliefs about what different kinds of digital communication are for, but in reality the majority can exercise only a small degree of choice regarding what they actually use. Most are restricted by cost and parental regulation from using many digital forms of communication, and given the platform-restricted nature of some communications – which is to say, you can only use BBM with someone also using BBM – are dependent also on what their best friends are able to use (which raises the rather disturbing possibility that children communicate most easily with peers who can afford the same level of media as themselves). Only a small proportion are sufficiently privileged to be in a position to choose freely between devices and communicative modes for their means of communication and networking. Many are made quite uncomfortable by the ways in which some of their peers display their wealth within the school context:

> I do have a phone, but not a smartphone. I don't like it when people with smartphones show them all the time.
>
> (Hannah, 13)

Limited choice, though, does not invalidate Livingstone's claim that young people make choices to some extent 'according to their distinct communication needs', so long as we accept that they are not necessarily making such evaluations with respect to a very wide set of options in most cases. While a few years ago Ito and colleagues described distinct patterns of use across the peer group – 'Teens will usually have a small

circle of intimate friends with whom they communicate in an always-on mode via mobile phones and IM, and a larger peer group that they are connected to via social network sites' (Ito *et al.*, 2008: 86) – our own evidence suggests that these things have become rather more varied and customised over time, even when the choices available for many are relatively limited. For many indeed, the only choices are between whether they use MSN or Facebook, both free, on their home computers, and in those cases they are not able to enter into digital communication when in school at all, while others around them are constantly passing the time in lessons by sending out messages to one another via BBM especially, although this particular form of communication is used within school to a large extent for rapid-fire exchanges, the majority of which are quite trivial, but which are nonetheless capable of inflaming social drama from time to time.

Social impact of digital media within school

Regardless of whether individuals are able to send messages when in school as well as when at home or elsewhere, and regardless of even whether they are in the very small minority that never engages in online social communication, everyone in the peer group might indeed find themselves caught up in some degree of peer group social drama, via one choice of medium or another, when they are in school (the following are from written survey responses):

> I like going on fb and msn at the same time but I prefer msn because I can just talk to people and sort stuff out rather than seeing all the rubbish on fb and spreading arguments to all of fb. also msn is safer as on fb people can see what your doing and fb is easier to add people.
> (Rakesh, 13)

> I think Facebook is a waste of time! It's a time consumer. If you're bored, you just go on Facebook to waste time. It also causes lots of arguments. Then people get involved when it's not necessary. Personally I prefer MSN to Facebook, I think it causes less arguments, and it's not annoying like Facebook. A lot of people update their status all the time. And people put very personal things on Facebook.
> (Lauren, 13)

> I think facebook causes arguments as if someone posts an upset or nasty status everyone suddenly gets involved.
> (Heather, 13)

In his study of the impact of Facebook upon 14–15-year-old teenagers' experience of social relations, Tope found that photographs underlay many instances of conflict, quoting one girl as saying that if tensions arise 'It's always photos . . . you can comment on photos . . . you wouldn't just start a fight on someone's wall, you'd [start] it over a photo' (Tope, 2011: 45). Tope suggests that the 'social confidence gained through the Facebook interface can too easily become a form of "overconfidence" that leads to rudeness and arguments' (ibid.: 51), and found that the lack of face-to-face contact made it easier both to get into conflict, but equally it was easier to develop new kinds of friendship, offering the individual 'varying degrees of concealment within the online social environment' (ibid.: 52). For some young people, the online and offline environment were felt to be 'different worlds', in which different social rules applied to some extent. On the other hand, the two worlds did touch one another from time to time, with disputes between two youngsters that had begun out of school on Facebook sometimes finding their way into classrooms: 'it's really awkward because they have supporters, and they have supporters, so there's just tension in the room' (ibid.: 45).

These conflicts, flare-ups and dramas are enacted in quite complex ways via the pages of Facebook, as the comments above clearly indicate. Marwick and boyd construct a quite specific account of what is signified by the notion of 'drama' encountered in particular in online social networking: an 'emic term used by both teenagers and adults to describe interpersonal conflict that takes place in front of an audience' (2011: 4). Drama as they describe it in this sense is a gendered phenomenon (seen as 'deeply unmasculine' p. 6) and, while not essentially dependent on online communication, benefits from the specific functionalities of Facebook:

> Alicia's story shows how the Facebook Wall can be used to demonstrate public support for one side of a conflict. A status message like 'oh my gosh I'm so over this' is intended to elicit support and feedback. Not only can friends respond with supportive comments, but they can also click the 'Like' button, which appears on each message to show their affiliation in an interpersonal interaction.
>
> (Marwick and boyd, 2011: 4)

These authors claim that being involved in drama is, 'in itself, a mark of popularity' (2011: 16). The male equivalent, among American teenagers at least, is characterised as 'punking and prankin', and in common with girls' drama, it blurs the line 'between what is hurtful and

what is simply funny' (2011: 22). Such drama constitutes an area of social intercourse among teenagers which, according to Marwick and boyd, is distinct both from gossip – which 'requires its subjects to be elsewhere', rather than often the instigators in the case on SNS drama – and bullying, which is more aggressive, sustained and enacted by instigators with some degree of power over the victim. For the most part, it seems that the conflicts, dramas, and playful aggression that most teenagers encounter or enact upon Facebook are not experienced as power-plays, and certainly we encountered few cases of behaviour that qualified as bullying in our own research (although we suspect that teachers in secondary schools increasingly find themselves fire-fighting Facebook-engendered dramas in order to allay parental anxieties about cyber-bullying).

But when bullying does occur, it is a completely different order of unpleasantness to the more common, largely playful arguing or niggling conflict between peers that dominates online communication, especially when in school. The cyber-bullying, especially via Facebook, that we did very occasionally hear about in our own research was serious and hurtful. As a rule, such Internet-based bullying is very often enacted out of school, as a means of extending situations of bullying that began in school to the whole of a victim's world. Such online bullying can sometimes prove very hard to stop once started for reasons specific to the applications being used. Aaron, 15, first told us about his experience of cyber-bullying in 2008, and in 2010 the problem had not been solved, despite concerted efforts on the part of his parents and the school. Aaron was known as an underachiever in school and had developed very solitary habits by the time he was 13: 'I did sort of always lock myself in the room and the only thing to keep me company was my laptop.'

Despite making sustained efforts to get out more and make new social connections away from the Internet, when he returned to his online worlds – which in some respects had been safe havens for him – he increasingly found himself exposed to inexplicable and systematic attack from some of his peers:

> I think personally on Facebook or MSN or even on phones for instance, the blocking system is no good. Because I've personally seen people go round it . . . I mean I've sat there before and they just do a group conversation [on MSN], because you can't block multiple people. So if there's two people that want to have it in for me and they're both blocked . . . they can just talk to me and I've got no way of stopping them . . . I can't really hide from it anyway, because even if I do block them, they got our phone numbers, you can't block them on phones and so technology sometimes . . .

you just don't want technology to be there. Like you want to . . . not the fact that I want to hide from technology, in some cases it's great, but in some cases you just don't want it to be like that. You want it to be a bit different . . . sometimes I believe that technology is taking away what it means to be human in some ways.

As Turkle points out, escape from the situation is not straightforward: 'You are stalked on Facebook but cannot imagine leaving because you feel that your life is there' (Turkle, 2010: 243). These experiences clearly meet the definition of bullying offered by Dan Olweus (cited by Darwick and boyd also) on his website:[5]

> A person is bullied when he or she is exposed, repeatedly and over time, to negative actions on the part of one or more other persons, and he or she has difficulty defending himself or herself.

The scale of online bullying described by Livingstone *et al.* in their EU Kids Online study (of 25,000+ 9–16 year olds) reflects our own experience of relatively small numbers. They found that 6 per cent of young people in this age group had been bullied solely online, while 19 per cent had been bullied both offline and online, indicating that more bullying occurs offline than online (Livingstone *et al.*, 2011: 6). Livingstone warns against over-sensationalising online bullying in particular, and recommends teaching children targeted by cyber-bullying a range of responses and coping strategies. For those children on the receiving end of specifically technology-enabled bullying, there is clearly a very special cruelty in exploiting the design weaknesses of resources that ideally reduce the isolation of already isolated young people. It is important, though, that such problems are not confused with the often hectic, sometimes stressful, but largely harmless behaviour taking place between teenage peers across the settings of school, the local neighbour-hood, and their online worlds.

New worlds, old worlds

> As if texting, swapping, hanging and generally spending their waking hours welded to their phones wasn't enough, 73% use social networking sites, mostly Facebook – 50% more than three years ago. Digital communication is not just prevalent in teenagers' lives. It IS teenagers' lives.
>
> (Henley, 2010: n.p.)

We started this chapter with the question of whether the Internet, and social networking in particular, is substantively altering teenagers' relationship to the traditional contexts of their adolescent years. Do these new and radically more available, radically more intensive forms of communication cut across the practices and values of traditional contexts in ways that forever change how young people experience them? Do they even constitute a whole new world – which adults cannot really see or enter for themselves – in which young people are growing up in new and different ways? This is certainly not far from what Livingstone (citing Gergen) suggests when she writes: 'Being "in touch" and "always on" allows children to be physically present in the home or school yet psychologically absent, engaged in the dynamic interplay of their social networks rather than family dynamics' (Livingstone, 2009: 91). She describes this level of engagement across digital networks as 'uninterrupted, unobserved immersion in peer communication' (Livingstone, 2009: 94).

Many commentators agree on the fact that access to these media is accorded great importance in their lives by many teenagers. Julia Davies, in her study of Sheffield 15 and 16 year olds, quotes one boy as saying 'You have to go on (Facebook) otherwise it's like you don't exist. If you are not there, then where are you?' (Davies, 2012: 15), which reflects danah boyd's observation in *Hanging Out, Messing Around, and Geeking Out* that 'For many contemporary teenagers, losing access to social media is tantamount to losing their social world' (2010: 79). Crucially, though, boyd goes on to moderate this claim:

> For most teens, social media do not constitute an alternative or 'virtual' world . . . They are simply another method to connect with their friends and peers in a way that feels seamless with their everyday lives. (Osgerby, 2004)
>
> (2010: 84)

However important digital media have become in the lives of many young people, they are nonetheless merely media: means of enabling and shaping the contact they wish to have with one another, and the things they wish to say to one another, as often and as much as they wish to; which, when it comes to teenagers, is a lot of time spent immersed in communicating. Digital media add particular kinds of value to the interactions that go on in those spaces, and offer ways of extending the communicative repertoire that they can draw on in a number of ways. The 13 years old referred to in the previous section are still figuring out what these spaces can do for them:

- I use Facebook and MSN quite a lot. I probably go on Facebook more often because you can chat, upload photos, write status etc. (girl, 13)
- I like talking to people on facebook that aren't in my year/at a different school. (girl, 13)
- I like Facebook. You can talk to anyone and also there's games on it so if I get bored I can play them. Also on Facebook you know when other people's birthday's are. (boy, 13)

These younger teenagers had at first been excited to be allowed on Facebook (on account of their relatively young age, and often through a deal involving accepting to 'friend' parents or other family), but most soon develop a rather more sanguine view of it: equal in pluses and minuses; a necessary addition to their social lives, but not so much fun as they had expected. Significantly, although offering genuinely new ways of managing what we might call the ongoing content of their lives, Facebook and other online social communications are not necessarily the source or medium for new kinds of content as such. Steinkuehler, quoted earlier in this chapter, talked of all the things teens were now doing with their digital media, but if you pause a moment and look at this list, it mainly speaks of those different media they use, and says very little about what those media might enable them to say: 'instant messaging, blogging, sharing files, consuming and producing media, engaging in affinity spaces, gaming, building social networks, downloading answers to homework, and researching for school projects and assignments.' There is not necessarily anything new in any of that.

This overlaying of old discourses and social behaviours upon new media[6] can be seen quite vividly in the case of young Japanese people using mobile phones. As the 2010 Pew Internet report on Teens and Mobile Phones by Lenhart and colleagues makes clear (in its subhead), the mobile phone is the 'centrepiece of their communications strategies with friends', via both voice and text, and increasingly a device for communicating via social network sites. This has in fact been the case for several years among Japanese youth, who had access to what were effectively smartphones years before youth in America or most parts of Europe. In her study of Japanese college students, Takahashi describes a quite complex set of uses of those phones that enable young Japanese people to enter new modes of communication while staying firmly within the parameters of social behaviour that have always surrounded them. The young people she observed used their mobile phones to manage two quite distinct forms of online social network as means of

both preserving and extending traditional Japanese modes of social relation: the core form of social group is described by the Japanese term *uchi*) signifying 'us' (the insider group of locality, school and college) as opposed to *soto*, 'them', the wider social network that reaches outside the close circle. The Japanese social network site Mixi was favoured for *uchi* communications, while MySpace was favoured for *soto* interactions. Most significantly, for her study, was the introduction of Mixi Mobile, which meant these youth could enact their social relations over their phones, a radically new opportunity at the time of her study.

Takahashi (2010) shows how the opportunity to use new technologies to facilitate these traditional forms of social relation allows the young people to extend beyond traditional social behaviours, without actually leaving them behind:

> While people participate in Mixi as a traditional uchi, to gain a sense of 'ontological security' (Giddens, 1990, 1991), they participate in MySpace to disembed from Japan uchi and have a chance to express themselves freely, away from the Japanese cultural norm. They reflexively create themselves through romanticizing images for participating in global popular culture communities, where MySpace can open up the soto world to them.
>
> (469)

In fact, far from offering some kind of digital alternative to the established adolescent world, the opportunity to access their online social networks any time and anywhere appeared to be a mixed blessing, exposing them to quite demanding social demands that had long been legitimised and expected within Japanese society. Takahashi, quoting Mori's comment (2007) that 'Japanese Mixi culture calls for a heavy commitment, and in many cases people feel choked by these thick relationships', points out that 'uchis do not only provide social intimacy, but also require the loyalty and commitment necessary for maintaining and reinforcing them'. For instance, she describes how these young Japanese teenagers feel under an obligation to show an interest in their fellow uchi members' diaries when displayed upon their mobile phone. Takahashi shows how Mixi Mobile allows young people to 'disembed from the immediate spatial locations to connect with their friends beyond time-space. They used it to reinforce social intimacy and maintain the *uchis* to which they belong' (2010: 459). The mode and medium of the uchis have changed or been expanded, but the social meaning of them remains more or less the same.

Summary

In her discussion of Massively Mutliplayer Online Games, Steinkuehler refers to 'the globally networked, technologically mediated, "figured worlds" (Holland *et al.* 1998) we now call home' (2009: 6), and while it is seriously exaggerating the case to say that we all now live in digital contexts, the ways that we weave our electronic communication into human space certainly has an impact on how we are in the traditional contexts of our lives. But while Sherry Turkle in *Alone Together* speculates that digital devices 'provide space for the emergence of a new state of the self, itself, split between the screen and the physical real' (2010: 16), she recognises that the central impact on young people is on the relations between the different people occupying that shared space, which in the case of teenagers most importantly consists of the home, and the family within it:

> when parents see their children checking their mobile devices and thus feel permission to use their own, the adults are discounting a crucial asymmetry. The multitasking teenagers are just that, teenagers. They want and need adult attention.
>
> (2010: 267)

As this chapter has shown, teenagers' uses of digital technologies clearly have a significant impact on life in the home, and are increasingly beginning to play a part in their lives in school too. These technologies enable and extend the kinds of social relationships and interactions that have always happened between teenagers in ways that are valued and valuable in their lives, but at a cost in terms of their capacity to attend to other things going on around them perhaps.

This chapter's question as to whether young people's uses of technology come anywhere near to constituting the emergence of a new and separate context of their lives is harder to answer with any certainty though, because we are looking at an unfolding narrative here, and one that is not about to reach a stable or definitive state. Tope's observation of the two worlds of teenage interaction is worth taking seriously, because of the suggestion that they act differently in their online world; less inhibition, with both good and bad consequences.

But, as the perspectives considered in the course of this chapter indicate, it would be an exaggeration at present to claim that teenagers' digital activities can be considered as separate contexts of their lives, where entirely different things go on, according to entirely different rules. Rather, we should see their online actions and interactions as a powerful element of their lives that is embedded within, and is helping to change, their existing contexts and processes of growing up.

4 Identity

Technology has for a long time been seen as an important part of supporting identity development among teenagers. In this chapter we consider how young people develop a sense of who they are, facilitated and sometimes stymied by the prevalence of new technologies in their everyday life.

> My mum is like a nature freak and my dad is like a technology freak. I think I'm a bit of both, so I'm like at war with myself.
>
> (Sara, 18)

The process of how we define ourselves can be understood from a range of developmental, psychological, social-cultural and historical perspectives (Kroger, 1996), and theories of identity vary significantly in the emphasis placed on these viewpoints (e.g. Stryker and Burke, 2000; Sfard and Prusak, 2005). Here, we define identity in a way that takes into account the interplay between these different dimensions. In simple terms, we view identity as how we define ourselves, based on our characteristics and attributes (our self-concept) and the social context(s) of which we are part (Alsaker and Kroger, 2006). Identity can change according to the contexts we find ourselves in and can also change over time. However, for most of our lives the different ways in which we define and present ourselves in the world, relates back to a relatively stable sense of self (Valkenburg *et al.*, 2005).

Adolescence is as an exceptional time for identity, as this is a period of life when young people have to find out 'who they are' within a context of multiple changes, psychologically, biologically and socially – the core interrelated foundations of identity (Erikson, 1963). The teenage years are a period marked by physical changes that result in both positive and negative emotional and physical experiences, and a greater cognitive capacity for self-awareness that changes a person's sense of identity.

At the same time, teenagers are trying to grow up, relying less on parents, making stronger relationships with peers, and trying to make choices about their future (Alsaker and Kroger, 2006).

This has never been a straightforward process but the development of a coherent sense of self is particularly difficult for teenagers in the twenty-first century. In the past, there were clear understandings of the role that a young person played in society. Yet, as society became more affluent young people, as we explained in Chapter 3, were no longer needed or expected to contribute economically to their society, and this has had the effect of making it more difficult for young people to make a strong connection to the world around them (Kroger, 1996: 4). In addition, there used to be a range of strong traditional markers of identity, such as, class, family, gender and location that supported the process of identity development. Yet now, while these traditional characteristics are still important, individuals can now make a far greater number of choices about who they connect with, how they look, and how to present themselves to others (Buckingham, 2008; Green and Singleton, 2009). At the same time as these two trends, current society is increasingly characterised by uncertainty, fragmentation and flexibility. New technologies have played an important part in facilitating the more transient, flexible and global set of choices that young people currently have open to them and have reconfigured connections to other people, places and ideas that can have implications for the development of identity (Bauman, 1998; Buckingham, 2008).

This chapter looks at the formation of different aspects or versions of teenagers' identity and the role that new technologies may play within this process. After discussing the connections between the online and offline world, in 'Performing identity' we examine how new technologies can allow or encourage young people to present themselves in certain ways online, leading to a range of opportunities for performing identity, in particular focusing on social networking and instant messaging. In 'Experimenting with identity' we consider how the Internet and other new technologies enable young people to experiment and play with their identity, while still based very much within the realities of the real world; and go on in 'Determining identity' to examine how young people can use the online environment to interact with others and access a wide array of material that they can draw on in defining their identity in relation to others and to technology. Identity is never static, and in 'Identity over the life course' we examine the role of technology in the development of a sense of self as teenagers group up. Finally, in 'Technological tensions' we examine the tensions present in all of these interactions, as technology can both support and complicate the development of identity.

First though, it is important to re-emphasise the connections between the real and the virtual, within the specific context of identity and technology.

Connecting contexts

In early research on the Internet and identity, many writers proposed that the online environment provided exciting and fundamentally new ways for young people to develop and play with their identities that were disconnected from the 'real world', enabling people to experiment with notions of 'who they were' in ways that were simply not possible in daily life. Yet, as we saw in Chapter 3, the online world is not entirely separate from the 'real', and more recent identity research has supported this view, highlighting that the Internet does not typically provide a space to develop multiple identities that are unconnected to the world and the person, but instead is another part or aspect that needs to be considered when understanding identity formation (Wynn and Katz, 1997). This is important, as it implies that the Internet does not lead to a radical change in our understandings of identity, or lead us to throw away previous research on identity development. That said, new technologies may offer young people some new opportunities and experiences, and it is those that we will focus on here.

In essence, we need to examine identity within a framework that understands how people interact online and how social vs. technical, real vs. virtual and public vs. private boundaries are (re)configured in online spaces (Wynn and Katz, 1997). Indeed, while there are significant methodological challenges of studying the development and negotiation of identity across different contexts (Leander *et al.*, 2010), many studies have demonstrated the importance of linking the online and offline worlds of teenagers (Merchant, 2012). For example, in a study of young people aged 11–16 in Britain, Valentine and Holloway (2002) demonstrate how identity is configured and negotiated within online and offline spaces, stressing that the online and the offline are connected. They highlight how online spaces enable young people ways to connect with others online, drawn together by interests rather than geography, and enable them to have more control over the way they come across to others or the way they position themselves. Yet, at the same time, these online activities tend to be very much situated within their everyday offline experiences. For example, by compensating for what they perceive as inadequacies in their everyday lives, building on or accentuating certain characteristics recognised and valued by their peers, and/or simply through their level or quality of Internet access, which is typically shaped by socio-economic factors (Valentine and Holloway, 2002).

The researchers also demonstrate how young people's online experiences are incorporated into the 'real' world, such as keeping in contact with distant relatives or maintaining friendships at school, or using online interaction to inform their real world hobbies, and talking about their online experiences with friends in class (Valentine and Holloway, 2002). Similarly, a qualitative study in the US demonstrated how young people used instant messaging primarily to connect with friends at school, and felt that knowing what went on online the night before was an important part of being part of the 'in crowd' at school (Lewis and Fabos, 2005).

Thus, in our understandings of identity the real and the virtual are closely related. When thinking about context, it is also important to consider other ways that the online space can be important for the development of identity.

Extending opportunities for personal space

I used to play the GameBoy when I was like, you know, I was a little kid. Nowadays I don't get on with games systems that well simply because of the amount of time they consume. It's like, you know, I'm over 18, the whole world is open to me. There's so much available now that when I was a little kid you know, out of maybe safety concerns or whatever, you know, you use your games, but nowadays [I hardly ever play].

(Kevin, 18)

As noted in Chapter 3, a key characteristic of current times is the extent to which young people's spaces are regulated, at school, in after school clubs and in the home, where parents might restrict the extent to which their children can go out and socialise due to concerns about safety. Such restrictions are likely to be problematic for identity development as young people possibly have fewer opportunities to interact and experiment with a range of individuals in social settings than used to be the case (boyd, 2007).

Thus, while technology is not radically transforming identity in terms of freeing people from the constraints of real life it does present a certain kind of freedom to young people where they can be themselves. It offers them a more private space away from the authority and control that young people experience in many aspects of their lives (boyd, 2007; Valentine and Holloway, 2002). For example, a qualitative study of young people's uses of MySpace in the US demonstrated that the social networking site 'facilitated emotional support, relational maintenance and provided a

platform for self-presentation where students could "be more relaxed", "mess around" and perform on their own terms with the social, cultural, and technical tools at their disposal' that was not possible within the formal constraints of school (Greenhow and Robelia, 2009a: 1153). Yet, it is important to recognise this level of agency within the wider social structures of which young people are part. This tension between young people's agency to operate in the online sphere and the home and school structures that shape the way they use technology was also apparent in a study of British teenagers aged 14–16, who explained that they used Bebo and MSN when they were bored, that is, unable to go out due to the control of their parents but with some level of agency over their Internet use (Willet, 2009).

Interestingly, this shift to the online world for socialising is to some extent supported by parents who actively encourage children to remain in the home; and typically justify the purchase of new technologies because of the danger of outside spaces as well as the educational role they are expected to play (Livingstone, 2007). Of course, this is not to say that the real world is no longer important. Indeed the bedroom as a space remains an important part of self-identity, in terms of how it looks, its valued contents (such as music, magazines, collectables) and being an escape from others where identity experimentation can take place (Livingstone, 2007: 315–6). Nevertheless, the less regulated nature of the online space is important to consider when thinking about identity.

Performing identity

As noted above, while writers differ in how they conceptualise identity, the social context is often seen as an important component, as this is where we present ourselves to others in some shape or form. Perhaps most famous in this respect is the work of Goffman, who provided a dramaturgical perspective on identity, arguing that we present ourselves to others in a similar way to an actor on a stage, with an awareness of the audience, norms and expectations the audience has (Goffman, 1959). While the direct applicability of Goffman's work to the online world has been critiqued and developed (Hogan, 2010), it is clear that the affordances of new technologies offer young people a range of different ways to present themselves online.

Indeed, the prevalence of social networking sites, and greater possibilities to produce and create images, audio and text online has certain implications for identity as young people are able (and to some extent expected) not just to use the Internet but to perform online. These more creative and social opportunities of the online world may encourage

greater reflection about 'who they really are' and how they want to be portrayed and viewed by others. In this section we look at the perform-ance of identity from two interrelated angles: social networking sites and instant messaging.

Social networking sites

The increasing dominance of social networking sites (which largely of course means Facebook at present) in the lives of the majority of teenagers involve them dealing with three key public elements – profiles, friends and comments – which all have implications for the performance of identity (boyd, 2007; boyd and Ellison, 2011).

The profile is one way for young people to signal to others their tastes and preferences and to convey their identity using various strategies. In her study of MySpace, danah boyd demonstrated how young people took time to learn the social norms of the site through observ-ing other profiles, prior to setting up their own, and then continued to develop their profile with great care (boyd, 2007). Indeed, similar findings have been found in later studies of MySpace, where typical strategies used to present the self included the use of photos, music choices, writing styles, page design and disclosure of information about important life events and affiliations with various people, tastes and attitudes. The setting up and development of a profile is done with a high degree of awareness of the audience and a conscious focus on a particular portrayal of identity (Greenhow and Robelia, 2009a).

Interestingly, for some, the profile is not used by teenagers as a direct way to convey themselves to others, via the provision of personal information, but instead is used to illustrate a particular role within the peer group. For example, in her qualitative study of young people's uses of social networking sites in Britain, Sonia Livingstone gives an example of young people who deliberately provide a jokey profile (with a funny picture, wrong age, and joke likes and dislikes) that they and their friends change. In using such a strategy a teenager is saying more about their fun, light-hearted personality and trusting relationships with their peers than using their profile to tell their audience personal details about their lives (Livingstone, 2008: 340).

Photos form an important part of this phenomenon (as indicated also in the extract from Tope's study in the previous chapter), as creating and sharing photos help people to construct their understanding of themselves and to present a story of themselves to other people (van House, 2009). In work that brought together four studies of people sharing their photos in various settings (both on and offline) van House highlights the

importance of performance within these practices as a way both to present a particular image or self to the audience (drawing on the work of Goffman) and as a way to enact the self based on the expected roles and norms for that individual to take on in a particular setting (drawing on the work of Butler) (van House, 2009).

Another key aspect of the identity teenagers choose to present on social networking sites is making visible their connections to others, as these are an important signifier about how popular or cool they are (boyd, 2007). This was a theme that was also apparent in our study, where the 'top friends' feature on Bebo often caused some level of anxiety:

> Some people . . . because you have like your top friends and um you can like pick who you want in it and where you want them, and some people get really into that. So it's like um oh where am I in your top friends blah, blah, blah . . . I think it's stupid [but] . . . you have to be like careful [with that].
>
> (Keri, 15)

Comments are also an important part of identity performance. These are used both as a display, for instance in commenting in certain ways on specific events, or in response to others and as a feedback mechanism. The comments from the audience is a way for young people to learn if the way they intended to communicate was successful or not, and in doing so they are engaging in impression management as proposed by Goffman (boyd, 2007).

The role of social networking sites in the development and maintenance of identity changes as young people grow up. This occurs both in terms of which social network site people tended to use, and how they use them. In the first year of our own study the social networking site of choice tended to be Bebo, followed by MySpace, followed by Facebook with older teenagers using Facebook more for communication and connections with friends and younger teenagers using it more to create strong profiles. Similar to Willett's study of Bebo (2009), young people are aware of the age appropriateness of the SNS site they are using. Our own findings were likewise similar to those of Livingstone, who suggests a move from 'identity as display' to 'identity as connection' as the values of the peer group change, and older teenagers recognise and rely on friendships more as they become more independent from parents and teachers (Livingstone, 2008: 402).

Indeed, as Facebook becomes more of a tool that young people have to use in order to be part of the group and in the know, we would propose that the role or importance of Facebook in the performance of identity

may be different depending on whether they are early or late adopters of the site. As some young people in our study seemed to use Facebook because they had to instead of really wanting to, we saw more evidence of 'identity as connection' as opposed to 'identity as display'. This could be explained because this first strategy tends to be less risky as it does not leave people as open or as vulnerable (Livingstone, 2008).

Instant messaging

Another tool that seems particularly important for the development of identity – particularly in the pre-teen and early teenage years – is instant messaging. Many of our participants gave interesting examples of how they used instant messaging to perform identity, holding multiple conversations at one time, deliberately controlling the pace of the exchange, sometimes copying and pasting conversations with one person into another stream and always trying to do so in a way that put them in the best possible light with their peers. As Lewis and Fabos describe in their study,

> participants enacted particular identities through IM: that they were busy, had lots of friends, were doing multiple things, and were interesting as a result. They would catch up, and then immediately fall behind as new windows opened and new conversations began that may or may not have affected the ones they were already having. They made some people wait to indicate their own popularity, while spitting out answers to others.
>
> (Lewis and Fabos, 2005: 489)

The use of instant messaging requires the performance of multiple identities at the same time; and it is this level of dynamic exchanges with multiple people that is perhaps significantly different to face-to-face interaction, which is also a performance but does not require constant shifting within the same time period (Lewis and Fabos, 2005). However, while the multiple performances in instant messaging can seem on the surface quite different depending on who is speaking to whom – there is a level of continuity. In their paper Lewis and Fabos give an example of a girl who in multiple ways communicates that she is a 'popular, in-the-know teen'. Yet she achieves this in quite different ways depending on the audience that illustrates her awareness of the specific needs, expectations and contexts of each conversation (Lewis and Fabos, 2005).

As well as active use of instant messaging, it played an important role in signaling 'hanging out' or simply being together in a virtual space.

For example, one 15-year-old boy in our study, Samuel, an extensive MSN user, said 'You sign in just to let everybody know that you are just there', explaining that 83 people were online at the time of the interview, but that only five would be ready to talk.

Thus, there are a number of ways young people can perform different identities online, with the affordances of social networking and instant messaging perhaps offering two key ways of achieving this in an online setting. Another important aspect of identity development is experimentation and it is this issue that we now turn to.

Experimenting with identity

> *So you think something different happens on MSN to face to face?*
> Sometimes. Some people are more confident on MSN and some people are more sick on MSN, and so obviously that is where the blocking facility comes in . . . yeah because I have a friend who met someone in her school [. . .] and they'd talk at school [. . .] he – she – they got her MSN, and they're in the same year and everything, and talk perfectly normal conversations in person and then at dinner they went on MSN and he started to go all sick and disgusting, and asking for all sorts of personal information. She was like what is going on!
> *And she was sure it was him?*
> Yeah yeah because of his webcam.
> *[. . .] that's pretty clear it's him then? Strange isn't it?*
> Some people are really strange . . . Yeah and she was just like okay. And she just deleted him and was just like, just leave me alone please? And obviously he did because he wasn't bad, but it was [. . .] I don't know what he expected really.
>
> (Emma, 15)

This exchange relates to an unsuccessful identity experiment. Identity experiments are seen by many as an important part of developing a sense of self. For a number of theorists the formation of identity requires young people to try out different (adult) roles to see what fits, and as part of this process sometimes role confusion occurs. The notion and importance of role confusion and identity was introduced by Erikson and later developed by Marcia (1966) (Alsaker and Kroger, 2006). While this work has been criticised, the majority of researchers interested in this area see some level of identity experimentation during adolescence as normal and important, and the Internet is one place where teenagers may do this (Valkenburg *et al.*, 2005).

The Internet enables young people to experiment with their identity in part due to its perceived anonymity and reduced auditory and visual cues (Valkenburg *et al.*, 2005; Zhao *et al.*, 2008). However, as noted above, online spaces are never truly anonymous (Lee, 2006), and the majority of online interactions by young people are linked with people in the 'real world' (boyd, 2007; Greenhow and Robelia, 2009b; Merchant, 2012).

Pre- and early adolescence tends to be a particularly important time for identity experiments. In a survey study in the Netherlands, of those young people aged 9 to 18 who used chat and instant messaging, about half the group engaged in some form of identity experiment, with younger adolescents being more likely to engage in these kinds of activities than older adolescents (Valkenburg *et al.*, 2005). Identity experiments can have a variety of purposes: in Valkenburg's study the reasons for adolescents to participate in online identity experiments were (in order of importance) to explore how others respond or react to certain behaviours (self exploration), to try and deal with issues of shyness (social compensation) and to facilitate connections with others (social facilitation) (Valkenburg *et al.*, 2005: 397).

Interestingly, while there were no differences in the amount girls and boys engage in identity experiments, they tended to engage in different kinds of self-presentation strategies, with girls pretending to be older or more beautiful and boys more macho. Such activities fit existing theories of adolescence where girls tend to mature earlier than boys, thus wanting to communicate with older people, and girls and boys conforming to traditional gender stereotypes (Valkenburg *et al.*, 2005). Similarly, in a qualitative study of mobile phone use by young Pakistani-British men and women, Green and Singleton demonstrated how men and women use mobile phones differently to perform and negotiate their own identities along traditional gendered lines, and in particular how men and women 'do friendship' using mobile phones in different ways (Green and Singleton, 2009).

Thus while, in some ways, the online sphere allows a certain amount of freedom and self-agency, these activities are carried out in a social context where young people are very much aware of social norms and the status quo, and tend to still conform or reenact these (Lewis and Fabos, 2005).

Personality is also important here, where in younger adolescents extroverts tend to be more likely than introverts to present themselves online as flirtatious and older, whereas in older adolescents the opposite is true, perhaps reflecting the challenges for introverts in the 'real world' as they get older (Valkenburg *et al.*, 2005). Indeed, other studies have

demonstrated the use of SNS to overcome shyness (Willett, 2009), and we also found evidence of this in our study:

> That's where things like Facebook come in because it's just so casual it's like it's really easy just to look on the Uni network and then find someone like from your course and just say, hey, you know, and you might make like a comment about the lecture or something. And then that in itself is just, because it's a very casual thing, I would never discuss something like deep on Facebook but it's really easy just to say, you know, how's it going, what are you up to. And because of that you can kind of get an idea of what other people are interested in without having to make sometimes a difficult step of actually just throwing yourself into a conversation where it could turn out that actually they're like the complete opposite to you.
>
> (Kevin, 18)

As is clear from these examples, the majority of these experiments remains very much fixed in the real world and shaped by existing norms and expectations.

Determining identity

Technology can play a part in how young people identify themselves, both in terms of who they are in relation to others and how they plan for and develop skills for their future selves. An important part of the development of identity is to be able to define oneself in relation to others (Spencer-Oatey, 2007). Identity is relational, and develops and is performed with clear recognition of those who are similar or different to the individual (Kehily, 2009: 7). Two aspects of relational identity are relevant here. First is how young people define themselves in relation to their uses of technology as compared to other young people, the kind of digital native discourse with which they are all familiar. Second is how, through a better understanding of their friends and other people they know, they can come to better understand themselves.

Being a geek

Young people's identity in relation to technology is perhaps particularly interesting, given the assumptions that many make about young people, that is, 'that normative notions of adolescent identity now include the desire for, if not facility with, digital and media technologies' (Lewis and Fabos, 2005: 495).

Drawing on the work of Martin (2000), Goode suggests that technology identity is made up of four areas of an individual's beliefs towards technology, consisting of views about skills, opportunities and constraints, its importance, and motivation to learn about it. This identity is developed via an individual's interactions with technology in a range of environments and interactions with other people (Goode, 2010). Individuals can vary in their technological identity in each of these four areas, and holding this identity influences how they continue to interact with technology and how they view themselves as individuals and as students (Goode, 2010).

> Every time I learn something new I always feel really good about it after. Like HTML and CSS is like a massive challenge because I think coding is fascinating. But people don't want to do it because it's boring.
>
> (Sara, 18)

Becoming an expert user of new technologies can be a particularly important part of the construction of identity by teenage boys, who are more likely than girls to base interactions with peers around specific activities (such as games playing and computer use) and thus like to demonstrate their expertise in these domains. Girls in contrast are less likely to demonstrate this expertise publically, due to the gendered assumptions of appropriate behaviour and tend not to base their friendships around specific activities (Facer *et al.*, 2001). Judith was well aware of her unusual geek status, although it was very important to her:

> Out of all my friends, it's quite strange, they're all mostly men um and I'm the computer geek [laughs]. And down the corridor I'm the computer geek. When someone got a Trojan at the beginning of the year I was the computer geek that was called.
>
> (Judith, 19)

However, geeks are still not cool (Valentine and Holloway, 2002). Many of our participants took care to be defined as not a geek, and some went as far to reject or reduce the importance of technology in their lives as far as possible:

> I never like spend a lot of time on like . . . well on the computer. That's a lie. I do spend quite a lot of time on the computer, I don't spend long on my PlayStation because I like . . . because sometimes teenagers get like really obsessed with them and I really don't want

to get like that because I enjoy reading and like socializing and like going out with my friends and stuff, and I don't want to be like a self-obsessed like computer freak.

(Lucy, 13)

Due to the prevalence of new technologies in the lives of young people, it is challenging for those individuals who are not particularly interested, do not really enjoy, or who have limited access to technology; as they have to try and develop their technological identity in ways that make sense to them. In her study in the US danah boyd found two groups of young people who were excluded from using MySpace. Those that were digitally excluded due to a lack of access to the Internet or high levels of parental regulation (see Chapter 6) and those who chose not to use it because they felt they were too cool for it, because it was only for cool kids or because they didn't like the News Corporation (respectively described in Chapter 2 as intermittent and ambivalent users). However, all had something to say about MySpace, which demonstrates the important role it plays in self-definition (boyd, 2007).

The second group of young people that were identified by boyd as not using MySpace due to explicit choices are consciously defining their identity in relation to the social networking site. Similar strategies to redefine identity have also been seen in cases where technology has been introduced into a workplace, and individuals have had to redefine themselves or adapt or address the challenges to their existing identity as a result (Nach and Lejeune, 2010). Integrating ideas from identity control theory (the work of Burke) with ideas from coping theory (the work of Pearlin, Lazarus and Folkman), Nach and Lejeune categorise different strategies for coping with the introduction of technology: these vary depending on whether the technology already fits relatively well with a person's identity or not (thus leading to a positive or negative emotional response) and where the response is negative, the level of control over a situation a person feels they have. While of course the case of young people is quite different from that of the workplace, the different ways that young people define themselves (as a mainstream, ambivalent or intermittent user of different technologies) is interesting and takes us beyond a straightforward assumption about 'digital natives' or the 'net gen'.

Understanding yourself in relation to others

One of my friends for example is a devout, too devout Christian. She's pretty born again so she gets me to look at some stuff and then

I will look a little bit further just because, I'm not someone that just because I'm not into it is going to drop it like indiscriminately. So part of it would be support and get along a little bit better, know where my friends are coming from just by kind of knowing what they're knowing.

(Kevin, 19)

An awareness of the audience is crucial in identity development. However, it is not just in terms of the feedback you get from your performance of identity or watching the performance of others (both on and offline) that matters. Another important role of new technologies is that it is a source of information. It changes the availability of information about alternatives or communities that you can belong to, which may not be geographically close by. It provides an opportunity to better understand the perspectives and lives of your friends and people you want to be like.

Other studies have illustrated the importance of new technologies for such activities. For example, a qualitative study of young people aged 17–19 from low SES backgrounds in the US highlighted how this group of young people used MySpace to find out more about their 'real life' friends (Greenhow and Robelia, 2009a). Furthermore, many young people who are not part of the majority of young people who use SNS or MSN are still likely to be using the Internet for identity formation through information seeking.

Identity over the life course

Just as it is important to understand the development of identity across all contexts a young person may encounter, it is also essential to understand identity as something that changes over time. As Kehily notes, a lifecourse perspective is necessary, as identity needs to be understood as a relationship between the present, the past and the future in order for us to work out who we are, what we do and what we will become (Kehily, 2009: 3).

Adolescence is characterised as a time of transition (Alsaker and Kroger, 2006). Transitions, such as leaving school, going to university, moving home or getting a job can mean a change in uses of technology and/or could represent a time when young people need to maintain or reconfigure their existing networks (Thompson, 2009: 12). When thinking about transitions, there are two broad aspects that are important. First is the sense of young people maturing, growing up, and moving on with their uses of technology and their changing priorities in their lives as the two comments below demonstrate:

I used to [use MSN] in year 7 and 8 but then since year 10 . . . work is starting to get a bit heavy now, so you're doing work on the computer and the conversations just keep popping up like 'hi how are you' from people that you've seen just at school, and it's like what's the point in this? I don't really use it at all.

(Emma, 15)

I won't be using Facebook as much when I leave Uni because it's all about Uni friends, having photos when you're going out, you know, it's quite personal but it's good fun. Like it shows the times you've had at Uni and everything . . . Facebook is like not really a special thing, so when I have to go out into the real work I have to have everything private, you know, not very many student photos up of me, keep it all sensible.

(Nyla, 20)

Thus, as young people grow up, their technology uses and the importance they place on different kinds of activities change in relation to the needs, expectations and goals they encounter or anticipate in their everyday lives – a process visible in embryonic form at least in the tentative explorations of the suitability of different communicative modes discussed in Chapter 3.

Second is the way that young people use technology to help develop their interests, helping them to work out who they are and where they want to go in the future. This is nicely captured by Greenhow and Robelia in their study of MySpace, who observed, 'Not only are students using *MySpace* for self-discovery, personal expression, and self-presentation, but also to clarify, showcase, and develop their interests and abilities within a network that values invention and sharing' (2009b: 132) and we provide some examples in our study in Chapter 5. An important part of growing up is for young people to take responsibility for their learning and to decide what it is they should learn in order to achieve their life goals (Illeris, 2003). Indeed, a number of theorists have stressed the important links between learning and identity, where identity is often viewed as a missing link between learning and its socio-cultural context (Sfard and Prusak, 2005).

As Erstad, an advocate of the learning lives approach, notes, this understanding must be considered in a longitudinal and holistic way, where learning is conceptualised as something that can happen in all contexts and over time (2011). Such a perspective highlights that people learn and use technologies throughout their lives both for and from situations that arise and are very much shaped by their personal social,

economic and networked contexts. Some of these situations can be moments of transition in the life course, such as moving from education to work, becoming a parent and so on; others are likely to be more subtle and at times perhaps even invisible to the individual at the time of the event (Biesta and Tedder, 2007; Erstad *et al.*, 2009). Key to the learning lives approach is agency, informed by past actions, present concerns and future plans.

Technological tensions

At times, the representation of young people's uses of technology can be quite rosy. Yet while new technologies offer a range of possibilities to support the performance and development of identity there are some challenges too. These have been reflected throughout the chapter – but there are two that are important to highlight here, dealing specifically with context collapse (boyd, 2007) and the permanency of the interactions online.

The complexity of the audience

I'll always like look through it [my Facebook profile] – but I always just think, what if my younger brother finds it? or what if my like younger cousin sees it? because I have them as friends and I am just like, well I am happy with it, there's nothing that anyone can use, to – like I don't have my phone number or anything on there, so I feel like it's pretty safe from anyone that goes on there . . .Yeah, because there are people that have like pictures and stuff, and it's just like, no! what if somebody sees it?! . . . I have pictures of me but people have, sort of, more pictures a bit – revealing I suppose. I'm just like, what if my mum sees it?! What would you do?!

(Rebecca, 15)

When people present themselves online, they do so with a sense of their audience that they themselves imagine and construct. Boyd draws attention to the need for young people to properly understand these different publics, but notes the complexity of this task (boyd, 2007). Young people have multiple publics, their parents, their friends, future employers and colleagues, who all differ significantly from one another (boyd, 2007). These separate and distinct groups in the real word are typically collapsed together on social networking sites. While young people are well aware of these multiple audiences (Lewis and Fabos, 2005), the conflation of these publics is still difficult to manage.

Young people tend to employ a range of strategies to deal with this 'context collapse', depending on the particular affordances of the social media site. For example, teenagers may reduce all portrayals to universally acceptable levels (such as in the quote above), use multiple accounts or alter profiles to make them more difficult to find. Indeed, in her study boyd found that teenagers employed a number of strategies to hide their SNS profiles from their parents, like changing their name or age, making profiles private, or creating a second account (boyd, 2007). However, problems remain, for example being seen to be authentic is important, but authenticity is determined by the audience in a particular context. Thus in social media sites such as Twitter where context collapse is prevalent, ensuring authenticity can be more challenging. But other techniques are possible here: such as trying to maintain a balance between revealing informative personal information and self-censorship (Marwick and boyd, 2011).

The permanency of interactions

> Sometimes I feel maybe some people might know a little bit too much about you . . . and it's like, sometimes your personal information can circumvent you. And that's not a worry as such but I just am not a big fan of that kind of ability.
>
> (Kevin, 19)

> Whatever you say on there can get back to people – if you say, if you sort of bitch about someone to a friend's face then they can't repeat it. If you repeat it, then that's not evidence, but lots of people have had where MSN conversations have been printed out and sent round the year, and so you got to be wary of that. Like, just one comment, even if you deleted if after, can be printed and shown. So basically, everything that provides evidence, so you've got to be wary of what you say to be people on there.
>
> (Rebecca, 15)

The permanence of online information is a relatively new and problematic phenomenon. Historically, forgetting was an important feature of all of our lives, enabling us to make mistakes and move on from these, but now forgetting is much harder to do thanks to the recording of all of our online activities. Furthermore, this is not always within an individual's control, and in our study many expressed concerns about the lack of control they had over the photos others added of them to Facebook and other platforms.

As Mayer-Schönberger notes,

> forgetting performs an important function in human decision-making. It permits us to generalize and abstract from individual experiences. It enables us to accept that humans, like all life, change over time. It thus anchors us to the present, rather than keeping us tethered permanently to an ever more irrelevant past. Plus, forgetting empowered societies to be forgiving to its members and to remain open to change. Digital remembering undermines the important role forgetting performs, and thus threatens us individually and as a society.
>
> (2009: 197)

Mayer-Schönberger goes on to point out that such forgetting is now almost impossible and the consequences of this are not yet fully understood. Clearly, for young people, who are almost required and expected to work out who they are via the use of technology, the permanency and public nature of a significant proportion of online information poses a particular problem.

Summary

Like all of us, young people are striving towards an optimum understanding of themselves, that they have a sense of 'this is me and this is where I belong' (Alsaker and Kroger, 2006). This chapter has illustrated that digital technologies can offer new ways to achieve this, from working out how to perform a certain aspect of identity, to experimenting with new or more grown up versions of themselves, to developing plans for their future selves. While the online sphere offers young people a space where they can have some agency over the development and representation of their identity, this is still constrained by the existing social and regulating structures that surround them. Furthermore, all of these opportunities hold risks at the same time (Livingstone *et al.*, 2011) – in particular, the risks of making mistakes or being misinterpreted by the perceived audience in ways that cannot be forgotten.

5   Learning

From their arrival on the scene, personal computers were credited with the capacity to change the ways in which children learn in schools, replacing the traditional passivity of classroom learning with 'an empowering sense of one's own ability to learn anything one wants to know' (Papert, 1982). In its 'Vision for the Future of ICT in Schools', *Transforming the Way We Learn* asserted that ICT, through appropriate and effective application, would enable 'pupils of all abilities to take greater control of their learning' (NGfL, 2002: 8). Reports from government agencies (e.g. Becta, 2003b) claimed as one of the key benefits of ICT, alongside increased commitment and self esteem, 'increased independence and motivation for self-directed study', suggesting indeed that the new levels of access to the Internet afforded by broadband connectivity would help pupils to 'explore independently and to achieve their own goals' (Becta, 2003a: 3).

To some extent: the institutions of formal schooling are also responsible for ensuring that young people learn the things that are required by the culture, and they are therefore understandably uncomfortable about losing too much control over how that learning is conducted. Schools' long-accepted authority over modes and content of learning is intrinsically at odds with the new world of free-ranging communication and interactivity that has grown up across online networks; a new world that has been embraced with particular enthusiasm by teenagers. The Internet, the most salient technology for learning, is not about to upset the hegemony of formal education, but neither does it support its power relations. Formal schooling has made controlled attempts to incorporate the Internet into its domain, but without much success, as if there is some kind of logical flaw in that particular enterprise (Cuban, 1993).

So where exactly should we expect to see substantial change in the ways that young people learn as a consequence of being able to use new

technologies? In this chapter, we shall look in two parts both at how the adult world has tried to direct the power of technology towards the learning of young people, and at how young people themselves make use of technology to support their learning.

In the first of these two parts below, 'Giving them what they need, False Starts' considers the technology industry's efforts over many years to connect with young people's learning. Then, in 'Necessary Evil', we consider various attitudes expressed towards educational uses of technology on the part of the adults who try to determine children's learning lives: government, schools and parents.

In the second part, 'Making their own arrangements', we shall look at how teenagers' opportunities for using technologies provide them with scope for learning of various kinds. In 'Using technology for formal learning', we consider the extent to which young people are able to benefit from access to technologies in and out of school for getting the work of formal education done to their satisfaction. Then, in 'Using technology for self-determined learning', we discuss how teenagers' self-directed uses of technologies enable other kinds of learning that reach beyond the school curriculum.

Giving them what they need

False starts

In 1945, Vannevar Bush, a scientific adviser to the US government during the second world war, outlined his notion of the memex, which is often cited as a model for the Internet. The memex was in fact conceived (but never made) as a microfilm-based device in which an individual could store and rapidly access all the knowledge they needed for their own particular lives. He saw the memex behaving like the 'intricate web of trails carried by the cells of the brain',[7] and in 'As We May Think' predicted that 'Wholly new forms of encyclopaedias will appear, ready-made with a mess of associative trails running through them ready to be dropped into the memex and there amplified'.[8] This notion of a web of knowledge provided a key metaphor for the Internet, and for the potential of what became known as hypertext and hyperlinks, and it contributed to the notion of technology enabling humanity to bring together all its accumulated knowledge for the benefit of future generations.

Shortly after, in 1948, the Disney Company introduced the term 'edutainment' to describe its True Life Adventure series. This series included semi-educational feature films (one of which became notorious for propagating the myth of lemming mass suicide), and the company

also produced educational cartoons, as well as setting up Tomorrowland, an educational section of the original Disneyland, in the 1950s, on to Epcot in the 1980s, dedicated to Walt Disney's personal vision to make science and technology innovation entertaining and accessible. This was characteristic of the age. Progress, embodied in the imagery of space travel and giant IBM computers, was a key notion in 1950s and 60s America. This imagery was ubiquitous in commercials, TV entertainment, cartoons and events such as the 1962 Seattle World's Fair, the Century 21 Exposition, celebrating the burgeoning new world of technology and commerce with its monorail and Space Needle (to the top of which, incidentally, local boy Bill Gates was taken aged seven). Computers came to be seen as providing the power and the magic by which we would attain a transformed world in the future, possessing boundless knowledge, super-human power and capacity for control (Sidoli, 2011).

Popular culture enjoyed an ambivalent relationship with computers during this period, fostering the long-established fear that the technology that humans build will ultimately destroy them. Computers and communications technologies were not surprisingly painted in a rather more positive light by the companies that sold them. Their educational potential was often a key marketing angle, as had been the case for every modern appliance at one time or another ('When television means so much more to a child than entertainment alone, can you deny it to your family any longer?') (Kosareff, 2005: 35). In the early days of personal computers the arguments for persuading people to buy were far from obvious, and education was clearly a market worth emphasising: 'Classroom of the Future'[9] from the General Telephone company in 1985, 'Connections: AT&T's Vision of the Future'[10] in 1993 (in which children learn at their own pace thanks to digital teachers), and the 'Future Classroom' video provided as an accompaniment to Bill Gates' 1995 book *The Road Ahead*, all offer the same fundamental promise that 'Learning by computer in the future will be fun' (Ardley, 1981).

Back in 1995, Microsoft marketed a series of CD-ROMs under the name of Scholastic's the Magic School Bus, which consisted of a series of educational animations on topics such as dinosaurs, wild nature and the human body, that claimed to be both fun and interactive, with a games element and excited children crying 'Where should we go next? It's up to us – WE'RE DRIVING THE BUS!' The focus on fun and independence became a familiar trope generally in the discourse for selling technology for learning to parents and children. AOL, without attempting to provide content, represented another strong corporate attempt to leverage the educational aspirations of parents on behalf of their children, offering to

mediate family users' entire online lives in the early days of the World Wide Web's expansion. One typical commercial, from 1996, opened with a flurry of modern '90s family life – high speed, gadgetised, manic – before settling on teenage girls clustering excitedly around a bedroom computer screen, looking at the familiar imagery of acceptable knowledge: dinosaurs, history, etc.:

> *Voice-over:* Do you know what's possible these days?! Conversations! Through your computer! Worlds of information – one click away! All the things you find, only on the world's most popular Internet online service, now more affordable than ever?! It's like living in the future. The future – now available on America Online![11]

Many other commercial concerns made their own attempts to gain a foothold in this market, many of which were undone by the dot.com crash of 2000–2001. Nonetheless, the corporate effort to deliver knock-out technological solutions for problems of learning is currently bigger than ever, even if this has not, according to the *New York Times*, convinced professional educators that such approaches really meet learners' needs: 'Amid a classroom-based software boom estimated at $2.2 billion a year, debate continues to rage over the effectiveness of technology on learning and how best to measure it' (Gabriel and Richtel, 2011: n.p.). Over the years, Microsoft in particular has continued to promote its case as a major player in the world of education, emphasising visually appealing, smart, and highly mediated means for accessing the worlds of science, nature, history and culture.

When it discontinued its own (for some time, highly successful) online encyclopaedia Encarta in 2009, Microsoft ensured its customers that nonetheless, it 'remains committed to delivering the most effective technology offerings to help make teaching and learning more engaging and relevant in the 21st century'. In fact, the corporation has become increasingly smart over the years about the need to work with and secure the trust of practitioners, and its Partners in Learning programme represents a substantial degree of progress over an earlier tendency towards highly mediated encyclopaedic knowledge, and somewhat Disneyfied representations of science and history. It is now focusing its provision via the cloud, making available useful free educational resources such as Windows Live SkyDrive and Learning Suite that have been developed for use in schools in partnership with professionals, and through investment in research.

Important as partnerships between formal education and companies such as Microsoft, Apple, Intel, Cisco and many others have been in

certain respects, though, the fact remains that corporations never quite seem able to gain the confidence of educators. Perhaps it is because they can never quite resist their discourses of triumph and wonder that somehow come across as hollow and insincere in the cautious and more downbeat settings of formal education. Even the greatly increased sophistication of Microsoft's current educational offer maintains the old hard-sell, promising to enable teachers to transform, inspire, create, empower, explore, share, and bring classroom presentations to life.[12] Technology has not yet been turned into fertile common ground for the very different cultures of commerce and education, but this is a massive market and we have certainly not seen the end of corporate attempts to leverage teenagers' affinity with technology in the name of education.

Necessary evil

In introducing the *National Grid for Learning* in 1997, the new UK government drew on the metaphor of the information superhighway, conjured by Al Gore in the early days of the Clinton administration, which itself strongly embraced the educational value of technology. Presenting the core New Labour information age rhetoric that 'children cannot be effective in tomorrow's world if they are trained in yesterday's skills', Tony Blair's Foreword promised that the NGfL would enable practically everything:

> It will help users to find their way around the wealth of content available over the Internet. It will be a resource for everyone in our schools. For example, a teacher will be able to get advice on effective ways of teaching children how to read. Pupils will be able to revise for their GCSEs or explore the museums of the world for their project work. Standards, literacy, numeracy, subject knowledge – all will be enhanced by the Grid . . . By 2002, all schools will be connected to the superhighway, free of charge; half a million teachers will be trained; and our children will be leaving school IT-literate, having been able to exploit the best that technology can offer.
>
> (DfEE 1997: 1)

This was quite evidently a highly ambitious programme and the UK government put a great deal of resource behind it (Selwyn, 2008). The thrusting optimism about the new world of universal digital skills implicit in the Blair government's vision might seem misplaced now in the context of the currently uncertain global economy, but the predictions of the importance of IT literacy have nonetheless proved accurate.

Fifteen years on, we take for granted the need for some degree of familiarity with technology and a readiness to develop new skills as an essential element of functioning in the modern world[13]: in its workplaces, marketplaces, cultural exchange, political life and social networks. Its place in education is, indeed, doubly assured: as an essential means both for functioning in the world after school, and for securing success in the formal education process as well.

Educators – teachers, policy-makers, senior management – clearly found it difficult, though, to articulate exactly what it was that technology was good for. Policy-makers had both to acknowledge its growing importance, while making it clear that traditional educational values were not at risk. Efforts to specify technology skills in curriculum documents tended to erase actual technology from the picture, to the extent that it is hard to imagine how or why anyone would wish to engage with it in formal education at all: the 1999 National Curriculum for England specified its ICT curriculum under headings such as 'Finding things out; Developing ideas and making things happen; Exchanging and sharing information; Reviewing, modifying and evaluating work as it progresses'. It is particularly striking that there was almost no reference to the World Wide Web or the Internet in the whole document, as if this was somehow not quite appropriate for something with the gravity of a national curriculum. Despite the earlier gushing talk of the information superhighway, the tendency most often was to keep technology, and especially the Internet, carefully at a distance, emphasising the importance of knowing both 'when and how to use ICT and where it has its limitations'.

This distrust reached into the home. As we indicated previously, many parents feel that they owe their children the chance to use a computer as part of their learning – 'it's an indispensible tool these days . . . I would want him to be confident with understanding the functionality of the core packages that are available' – while somehow regretting that they were doing so:

> You know everybody's going to have a laptop in the future, everyone's going to be doing everything on laptops. I'm not necessarily sure if I think that's good, but I think that's the way society, our country, especially this day and age is going to go.
>
> (Mother of Stuart, 9)

> I want her to use the technology but I also want her to be aware you know of what else is out there for her education.
>
> (Mother of Debbie, 16)

There are two sides on the computer, positive and negative.

(Father of Habib, 14)

I'm sceptical about the quality of the information which can be found on the Internet which is why I will always go to a book first, if we have it on the shelf.

(Mother of Monica, 9)

As home access to the Internet expanded, public anxiety about the Internet also became increasingly focused on issues of safety online:

I find it quite scary really . . . I've seen too many programmes of how paedophiles find children that way and it scares me . . . I've told her exactly in constant detail in what exactly they do and how they can trick her into giving information and things like that, so I think I've scared it out of her now.

(Mother of Anna, 9)

While there is no doubt that many young people act in quite hectic ways online, the focus on issues of sexual predators and inappropriate online relationships has possibly had a disproportionate impact on how many adults and young people regard the Internet. The combined effect of warnings, from both school and home, about the multiple dangers of paedophiles, viruses and unreliable knowledge sources left quite a few people feeling that the wealth of knowledge expected from Internet access were something of a mixed blessing. Add to this the danger of cyber-bullying, and it seemed to be the case, by the time the Byron Review came out in the UK in 2008, that the indispensability of the Internet was disputable. In 2011, the *New York Times* ran an article about a Waldorf School, for the children of Silicon Valley executives (eBay, Google, Apple etc.), which has entirely repudiated technology for learning:

. . . the school's chief teaching tools are anything but high-tech: pens and paper, knitting needles and, occasionally, mud. Not a computer to be found. No screens at all. They are not allowed in the classroom, and the school even frowns on their use at home.

(Richtel, 2011: n.p.)

Reasons given include the argument that teaching is a human experience, technology is a distraction from the things that really matter, such as literacy, numeracy and critical thinking, and is now so easy to

use that there is no need to learn to use it when young. As arguments not founded on actual evidence go, these are no worse than the cheery technological determinism (Selwyn, 2012) of the pro-technology arguments deployed in a previous *New York Times* article: 'digital devices let students learn at their own pace, teach skills needed in a modern economy and hold the attention of a generation weaned on gadgets.' But efforts to leverage the benefits of new technologies often amount to using the immediate attractions of new media in order to preserve highly conservative notions of education, as evidenced by the videos from the Khan Academy on YouTube (slogan '89,439,453 lessons delivered') (Sengupta, 2011), which straightforwardly deploy blackboard-style exposition and transmission of knowledge, but in what is claimed to be a personalised way (because the learners can watch the videos on their own devices). It is possible that these approaches do afford learners some degree of choice over where, when and how they access the knowledge on offer, but there is little evidence of any change to the traditional relationship between teacher, learner and knowledge.

Such approaches only minimally engage with what we see as the central issue here: the ways in which young people, through the increased agency that digital technologies are presumed to grant, are able to get to grips with both traditional and new forms of knowledge in new ways, and on their own terms.

Making their own arrangements

While we must be careful not to exaggerate the natural intuition or unwavering enthusiasm of teenagers for using technologies, it does seem that this is an area of their lives where they feel more than usually able to exercise significant amounts of self-determination and choice, within the crucial wider contexts of family, school, friends and mass media (including the Internet). In this section, we look at the extent to which the uses of technology for learning are thus driven by the young people themselves, both in terms of how these support school learning, and non-school learning of various kinds.

Using technology for formal learning

It has been argued for a long time now that schools offer what is to some extent a restricted service in terms of access to technology, and the Internet. Over a decade ago, Buckingham (2001) showed that compared with the exhilarating experience of multimedia outside school, many children complain that use in schools is far too limited and restrictive.

Facer *et al.* conclude in *Screenplay* that over-prescriptive and linear practices limit school-based learning of ICT (2003).

Experiences of technology for learning in school are variable though. Some secondary school students were positive about the ways in which their teachers incorporated specialist tools and software into their learning – 'Computers are like a main thing of the school really. They help to advance learning in a more vibrant way' (Liam, 15). Students reported using complex software such as Microsoft Macromedia and Dreamweaver (for website creation, particularly in relation to one of the 'business' lesson modules) and Flash (for 2D animation creation); Movie Maker (for videos to be included in their webpages); art software such as V2 (for a product design class); and Microsoft Publisher (for creating magazines and publication materials for the media option), especially within GCSE options where they engaged in activities such as 'product design' and graphics option classes.

For reasons of both cost and lack of information about appropriateness, opportunities to benefit from specialist software in the home are rare to non-existent. Instead, the educational software used in the home is mainly limited to core applications from the Microsoft Office range, serving two main purposes – to consolidate basic skills, and to prepare classroom presentations (uses that can be tracked directly back to the hi-tech corporation videos from the 1990s promoting the educational value of their products):

> *Give me an example of the sort of thing you might do on your computer for your homework?*
>
> Um, using Excel to put tables and use it for graphs. Word, sometimes PowerPoint
>
> (Trevor, 16)

This leaves the Internet as the single most valuable (if also most contested) learning technology in the home. This has become increasingly the case since the widespread arrival of broadband connectivity; using the Internet is normally far easier in the home than at school, especially because of in-school Internet filtering, and problems of access. Researching topics through the Internet at home has become a staple of the formal learning technology repertoire, both because many homework tasks explicitly require it, but also because the young people themselves rely on the Internet in order to fill in gaps in their knowledge: 'Yeah I'd use the Internet, Wikipedia whenever I need to, or I feel I need to' (Nick, 14). This of course immediately raises the problem of teaching them to be discerning users:

How do you use the Internet for homework? Um just basically Google or Ask, and then type in what I need to find out and find out sites, and read the, you know, find out what I need to, ask what I want to know. And basically copy and paste then edit it and, you know, make it my own.

(Samuel, 15)

There is no doubt that learners get to carry out some reasonably worthwhile learning tasks this way, as well as working online with a few instances of subject-specific software such as MyMaths. It might also be argued that, despite sometimes enabling indiscriminate downloading of content for pointless homework projects, such access does provide all teens with a valuable way of filling in gaps in knowledge, and answering questions they would not otherwise be able to answer, to some extent moderating the disadvantage between those with ready access to school knowledge, and those without. Jamie, a 13-year-old mainstream teenage technology user, considers his computer the most valuable technology in his life, because 'without it I wouldn't be able to do like home-work and stuff, and I wouldn't be able to go on the Internet'. 'Finding the stuff' on the Internet is, as far as he is concerned, his major skill with technology.

There is no question about the fact that technology and Internet resources are now used in much of the formal education work done at home as a matter of course, especially in the early years of secondary school. Some older students tended to limit Internet dependence when it came to preparation for life-defining public examinations in the final years of school. It is at this stage, more than any other, that it seems that the knowledge wealth of the Internet is perceived as unreliable with respect to the specific requirements of the formal examination syllabus, and is avoided in favour of more bounded sources:

making notes through the textbook there, and then when I'm making revision notes I go from the revision guide, and then if I'm confused about anything I go back to textbook if I am still confused go back to my teacher. That's how it works . . . and then sometimes if I'm confused at home, when I'm stuck there, I'll go Google it in – like help! What do I do with this question? so you like go to your room where your laptop is to Google it and then come away from it.

(Jasmine, 16)

We have assigned textbooks for each subject, we're normally given a worksheet using the textbook, which is focused on the material

we're doing. I rarely use the Internet, unless I was really searching for something I wanted – sort of a second opinion or different information, I'd use the Internet.

(Nick, 17)

With respect to formal learning, it seems that the Internet serves most of all as a reassuring quick fix for teenage learners. We have already noted how the provision by Google and Wikipedia of instant answers to informational difficulties to some extent ameliorates the problems of studying largely in isolation at home. In these respects, the continuous presence online of peer support networks is also vital for many, used as a matter of course by the great majority of teenagers. We found little evidence to suggest that much sustained or substantive collaborative knowledge construction was taking place through these forms of online communication – online chat, social networking site, email, and various combinations of all these – but it was clearly the case that these performed an important problem-solving service, at the level of clarifying homework tasks and resolving minor difficulties:

it's when you type it up and you've only got like a couple hours to do it, then re-read, it just sounds right, but if you send it to someone else it might not sound right and so they can like give you a pointer.

(Milly, 13)

What happens at home if you get stuck with anything; who helps you there? I normally talk to my friends on MSN about it all or just remember what I did in the lesson and just go back through it and stuff. Or just do it and then just do something at it and like try.

(Suzy, 13)

all the time. Especially helpful with homework. I think maybe ten years ago you'd phone a mate up and copy it down, but now – just on Facebook.

(Nick, 17)

Even Jas, who steered clear of the Internet while doing formal schoolwork, recognised the reassurance value of being able to call on friends online when she could not think of a word she was looking for:

I will do that when I need to – I'll just type in whatever question's on my mind because, you know, you can put your Facebook status and ALL your friends will see that, so . . . It could be anything,

absolutely anything ... I'll put it into Facebook and I'll get like fifteen comments, different words.

(Jasmine, 16)

School is not yet a major active player in their online learning lives, but where teachers have the time, opportunity and confidence to provide online guidance and structure for homework activities (which themselves are structured around Internet-based content), the school learning platform becomes rapidly integrated into young people's home study routines:

you need it for research and to type things up and to access quite a lot of homework from the Internet ... I think it's good ... it's kind of there for you so you can see all your grades and all what you've done, you can go back onto those homeworks quite easily.

(Joseph, 15)

Such opportunities provide a kind of balance between learner and school, so that one might envisage some degree of shift towards the agency of the learner, for instance in enabling some degree of dialogue between teacher and learner. It was clear from some, though, that the idea of anytime anywhere learning (much promoted in the early days of broadband) has not yet extended to an expectation of the teacher being available online:

You would never be in touch with your teacher about your homework?

Why would our teachers give us their numbers? They'd never do that. No! Our teachers would never give us their numbers!

(Fiona, 14)

It has turned out that formal education has developed its technology practices on a different timescale from that envisaged during the early days of the digital revolution, when we were promised the rapid introduction of superhighways and national grids for learning. Progress towards the purposeful integration of technologies into school practices continues to advance, one step at a time, as those practices are gradually adapted in order to absorb the somewhat intrusive presence of screens and the Internet into the teacher–pupil relationship. It has proved to be a quite sluggish process, and the young people themselves cannot help moving faster than this. Even in their uses of technology for their formal learning, it is the students who tend to take the initiative, sometimes

initiating behaviours that would have been unimaginable even three years ago. Sean, 18, describes how one of his A level (18+ examinations) teachers allows the students to use their own devices to access the Internet in his lessons (an embryonic version of the BYOD approach described in Chapter 3):

> if you've got a smartphone in class, and they explain something, you can always look it up if you don't quite get it, on your phone there and then.
>
> (Sean, 18)

He goes on, though, to wish that school would be more proactive than this in incorporating technology – 'they should take the initiative' and Nick, also doing his A levels, notes that 'They [teachers] don't actively encourage . . . but they don't discredit it either'. The landscape of their formal learning is certainly changing, though at nothing like the pace that occurs in other kinds of technology-related learning.

Using technology for self-determined learning

Here we are referring to anything other than what is determined by the school curriculum, and which happens as it does because technology is significantly involved. This encompasses the teenagers' generally positive – because substantially self-directed – experiences of finding out how to make technologies actually work for them, and the extensions of this into creative explorations and activities that are both enabled and made specially meaningful by technology. It seemed to us that such learning often turned out to show a confidence and inventiveness that was seldom apparent in the ways that these same teenagers used technology to support formal learning.

Before looking in more depth at such instances, we should note the few instances we came across of teenagers using technologies in line with the wonder of knowledge paradigm. In effect, these instances were a kind of hybrid between formal and self-determined learning, in which learning behaviours adopted from formal education were applied to self-selected learning topics. These included looking things up ('I occasionally research things which come into my head, mainly questions about physics or space'; David, 15), keeping notes, trying to engage in 'classified' (Furlong and Davies, 2012) learning such as one boy's failed attempt to learn Russian online, or exploring future career possibilities: 'I'm trying to be an architect so I go on the Internet and see what you have to do further to be an architect' (Leila, 13).

For the most part, this kind of earnest self-directed engagement with adult conceptions of the knowledge their children might gather from the Internet appeared to be short-lived and unsatisfactory when it was attempted, and that was seldom. More than anything reflecting the image of learning offered to parents in ISP adverts, they did not reflect what was valued or desired by the young people themselves, who were rather more concerned to find out how to increase their control over technology so that they could do the things they wished to do, and take their place in their peer group technology and online sub-cultures.

'We just learnt on the go really'

Thus, the kind of technology-related learning we saw most from virtually all the teenagers in our sample, mainstream and enthusiasts alike involved their processes of actually learning about using technology: it is the form of learning about which they seem to be most articulate, and aware. The picture that emerged strongly reflects the wider realities of adolescence: in terms of how they engaged with technology, learnt to use it, and used it for learning, the young people we saw were determined to find their own ways of doing things, while drawing freely on whatever help available might make that possible. As the comment above from 15-year-old Alex indicates, this kind of learning is experienced as something quite different from school learning: light, alert to new needs and possibilities, easy because shared.

Play and necessity are indistinguishable here: for many of these teenagers the satisfaction lies specifically in working things out for themselves and discovering new tricks, finding themselves very often on equal terms with the adults and experts in their lives as they do so.

It just seems easy, it's just like press stuff and it works.

(Samuel, 15)

You just pick it up really . . . as you go along, just work out [. . .] Just like, play it by ear I guess. See stuff and you go, oh what does that icon do – trial and error really.

(Nigel, 15)

She's [sister] asking how to do such and such, how do you start the text message, how do you add a number to the phone book? And it's like I know and let her get on with it. Explore it for herself. Never take the fun out of exploration. [laughs]

(Nessa, 16)

Much of the key learning of basic technology skills has begun long before the teenage years, and the evidence of our own research showed clearly that the learning curve for such learning was as steep for most pre-teens as for much older people: their particular capacity to learn to use technologies was internally driven by strong motivation, but dependent on access to knowledge and direction from others. For these younger children, this involved a combination of unstructured experimentation, varying degrees of family support and encouragement, and important early encounters with technology in school:

> Yeah it was my dad that taught me how to use it. I just saw him typing on it and I came over and said, can I have a go? . . . and then when I came to [primary school] we started to get to know the computer.
>
> (Sheila, 9)

> I learnt to use Word [. . .] I learnt Word from my uncle a bit, and then I figured out the thing a bit more myself and then from the school, figured out.
>
> (Deepak, 9)

> when I was little, my cousin like told me how to get on to like the Internet and everything. But since I came to school I have learned a lot more.
>
> (Jackie, 9)

As they advance through the teenage years, those initial forms of support are augmented or replaced by peer networks, which increasingly determine technology preferences (for devices, games, choice of social networks and communication channels), orientation of various kinds towards technology, and the opportunity to participate in a community of shared knowledge and interests. At the same time, as teenagers move through secondary education, school seems to lose credibility as a source of technology expertise. Unlike the earlier years, technology instruction at this stage was often viewed as being irrelevant and inappropriate to their needs by a considerable number of the technology-confident main-stream teenagers we spoke to:

> they just teach you like stuff, like formula for Excel which you could just like go onto a web page and just read. And they spend like five weeks teaching you that, and it's just like, what's the point? It's just stupid.
>
> (Dominic, 15)

they're always quite basic but you also have to do a lot of it just to show you can do it, you have to show you can write a Word document – and I'm like 'no I can do that, I want to do the other stuff!' and it's a bit like 'no but you have to show it' so that gets frustrating and like, show you can open an email and I'm like 'I can do it! I'm 15!'

(Rebecca, 15)

The efforts of formal education to teach teenagers about technology have until now connected quite poorly with the things that interest and preoccupy them most, and nor do these seem to offer a way of building on the skills and understandings they are potentially developing through their social networks and other online engagements. In their major report for the MacArthur Foundation, Jenkins and colleagues explored what these interests and preoccupations potentially signify, within the context of what they refer to as the new participatory cultures within which teenagers are growing up. Referring back to the Pew Internet and American Life project's finding that 'one-half of all teens have created media content, and roughly one-third of teens who use the Internet have shared content they produced', Jenkins *et al.* propose that:

In many cases, these teens are actively involved in what we are calling participatory cultures. A participatory culture is a culture with relatively low barriers to artistic expression and civic engagement, strong support for creating and sharing one's creations, and some type of informal mentorship whereby what is known by the most experienced is passed along to novices. A participatory culture is also one in which members believe their contributions matter, and feel some degree of social connection with one another . . .

(Jenkins *et al.* 2006: 3)

The report argues that there will be considerable benefits for those who learn to operate effectively within this culture of participation, such as new essential skills of collaboration, more open attitudes towards knowledge, greater scope for cultural expression, skills for the new workplace, and more empowered citizenship. Identifying a cultural shift from individual expression to community involvement, the authors outline a number of specific new media literacies that mostly 'involve social skills developed through collaboration and networking':

- Play – the capacity to experiment with one's surroundings as a form of problem-solving.

- Performance – the ability to adopt alternative identities for the purpose of improvisation and discovery.
- Simulation – the ability to interpret and construct dynamic models of real-world processes.
- Appropriation – the ability to meaningfully sample and remix media content.
- Multi-tasking – the ability to scan one's environment and shift focus as needed to salient details.
- Distributed Cognition – the ability to interact meaningfully with tools that expand mental capacities.
- Collective Intelligence – the ability to pool knowledge and compare notes with others toward a common goal.
- Judgement – the ability to evaluate the reliability and credibility of different information sources.
- Transmedia Navigation – the ability to follow the flow of stories and information across multiple modalities.
- Networking – the ability to search for, synthesise, and disseminate information.
- Negotiation – the ability to travel across diverse communities, discerning and respecting multiple perspectives, and grasping and following alternative norms.

(2006: 4)

The authors of the report argue that teenagers are not necessarily going to acquire such skills on their own simply through interacting with popular culture. Arguing that the possession of these skills will be essential for success in the future, the report asserts that 'Everyone involved in preparing young people to go out into the world has contributions to make in helping students acquire the skills they need to become full participants in our society' (Jenkins *et al.*, 2006: 4). The report, indeed, goes on to explore how this might be done (specifically within North American schools), offering many examples of how the curriculum could accommodate and make use of relevant practices. The aim, presumably, is both to put young people's existing practices to some use within formal learning contexts in order to enhance curriculum learning (such, for instance, as Edmodo[14] is attempting to do, in trying to bring the look and feel of Facebook into schoolwork), at the same time enhancing digital/new media literacy learning more widely.

There are, in fact, two separate issues to be considered here: are these skills as important as the report claims, and is the report correct in arguing that it is the responsibility of formal education to ensure that they are learnt?

The nature of digital skills

At first sight, the skills as formulated in the MacArthur Report go beyond purely common sense descriptions of what young people might do and learn in their uses of technology, and in some respects are as abstracted from specific technology skills as the National Curriculum descriptors which were criticised earlier in this chapter. On closer reflection, though, they prove to be very effective in helping us to focus on the kinds of things that young people actually do, in developing their own uses of technology for various purposes on their own initiatives and in their own ways. As such they reflect the key theme of the present discussion of the learning associated with teenagers' uses of technologies: that the most effective kinds of technology-related learning is arguably that which is generated and devised by teenagers themselves.

The previous section suggested that all teenagers to some extent figure out for themselves, in collaboration with their personal networks, how to use technologies for their own purposes. The examples below demonstrate how some teenagers are able to develop more sophisticated uses of technology in the course of following their own interests and collaborations, resulting in opportunities for learning multiple digital literacies and skills that closely match those outlined by the authors of this MacArthur Report. Even the technical business of coding a web-page carries much wider meaning if we see it as enabling a more effective presentation of self to others, known and unknown, within a social networking site:

> you see someone's like page on MySpace and it looks really good, and you think, how did they do that? And so, and then you learn to do it yourself . . . because you use HTML for all the pages, I learnt all that from websites. They just told you about it. So I learnt a lot then.
>
> (Rebecca, 15)

She is engaging here in what Jenkins *et al.* designate play and appropriation, in this case experimenting with and appropriating the specific technology skill of coding with HTML in order to establish an online identity within a social network that allows for some degree of individuality. Focusing on his own technical learning in a similar way, 15-year-old David talks of learning to use a particular form of coding in order to design games, which both enables him to explore his own design skills, and to participate actively in an online community of designers. In such activity it is possible to detect evidence of the development of distributed cognition, collective intelligence and networking:

I do know one programming language. Not sure if it's the most useful language . . . it's a version of Assembler . . . I use it for editing things in certain games . . . for example how enemies behave or making new ones, a pretty simple platform game. Then you go on to a forum to discuss these things.

(David, 15)

Thinking in terms of these skills also allows us to see the ways in which highly active teenage technology users develop and blend different skills as they connect offline activities with online, moving as they do between different communities and activities – technical and aesthetic skills of photo-editing, selecting appropriate online sites, engaging with different communities, and through gaining both a sense of self-efficacy and identity:

I have like this account on this thing called DeviantArt and it's like a big art thing and you can do . . . and everyone's got a page on it and like just upload all their art. And you can just like look at it all and it's like a really, really nice club . . . it's like really, really good.

(Keri, 15)

In Jenkins *et al.*'s use of the term, we could describe the way she moves between different networks – her offline/online local social group and the online distributed interest group that she has just joined as a good instance of negotiation, and we could also point to specific signs of collective intelligence, distributed cognition, judgement, and networking taking place. In a slightly different way, because exemplifying a kind of group movement between activities, rather than a solitary individual connecting with different groups, Samuel's account of his group dance and video activities (from Chapter 2) demonstrates a wide, and quite complex, range of activities that seamlessly integrate the offline and online worlds of this teenager:

on YouTube there are hundreds of thousands of videos . . . you put it onto Bebo, on your own webpage, so that your friends will come and see it, and then they'll upload it onto their Bebo, it's by one click, and then other people will see it and you'll become famous . . . then we started, you know, learning more dances and making whole choreography dances, going for competitions and we got really known. So, yeah.

(Samuel, 15)

Added to similar instances of distributed cognition, performance, simulation and collective intelligence, one can also point here to this as an example of what the report calls transmedia navigation, in the way that these youngsters choose to represent their dance activities online, and make rationalised choices between YouTube (near certainty of being lost in the crowd) and Bebo (near certainty of high impact within the local community).

The final example of skilled participation in online worlds concerns Trevor, a 15-year-old boy who in 2008 was spending several hours, often late at night, communicating – often simultaneously – in a number of different communicative modes: MSN, Skype chat and Skype video. He was very clear about the communicative skills that he and his friends were developing online, an example of collective intelligence that Trevor holds in high value, in summing up what he feels he is gaining from his online life:

> I think you learn to be more safe of yourself; you learn to be more protective. You learn to be more social. Um, you learn loads of things. I mean you . . . of course you learn, you get better knowledge and stuff, and so it all comes down to that.
>
> (Trevor, 15)

There does seem to be quite a range of different complex digital skills being constructively learnt here, in the course of self-determined activities that are primarily undertaken for pleasure and interest, all of which suggest that the notion of the participatory cultures does indeed figure in these teenagers' lives. While we would not claim that the MacArthur Report formulations necessarily offer the only or best ways of naming the skills involved (the wording of some seems less than intuitive at first sight, e.g. 'Networking – the ability to search for, synthesise, and disseminate information'), they do an important job of helping us to focus on ways in which we might take some of the quotidian technology-related activities of young people considerably more seriously than they might normally be taken by adults and the popular media. But the examples above do not necessarily reflect the full picture of what young people more widely do and learn in the course of their lives online, and whether they would want to, given the appropriate guidance or encouragement.

Can such skills be taught?

The argument that all young people should be helped to gain the skills and understandings appropriate for the new participatory cultures is not

as straightforward as it might at first seem, for a number of reasons. First of all, these are not skills to be taught the way one might teach scientific knowledge, or literacy skills, or a foreign language. Rather, they are practices inscribed in everyday life that have developed through collaborative interactions within specific cultural and social groups. Such practices are not likely to thrive when taught or exemplified on the basis of general principles, but rather need to be fostered and understood in the worlds in which they prosper, which are non-formal, non-hierarchical and non-institutional. In these online worlds, behaviours are formed iteratively and experimentally, reinforced by the unique socialisation processes of the Internet, and constantly subject to rapid change.

This is not to say that the practices, social behaviours and literacies of online networks are not a proper subject for sociological and cultural analysis, in school or anywhere else. Schools arguably could embrace opportunities for young people to articulate, share and examine the implications of the things that they encounter and do online. It is important too that social institutions should address issues of digital exclusion, which partly should involve schools providing opportunities for online interactions denied elsewhere, although this is not an issue to be addressed generally in classroom teaching so much as for the promotion of specific policy solutions (such as the UK Labour government's Home Access scheme, which provided Internet connected laptops for economically and socially disadvantaged young people).

Achieving such goals is not, ultimately, part of the agenda of schools, which are of necessity more concerned with epistemological than ontological processes, and these kinds of digital literacy skills are less about the accumulation of knowledge than about how you engage, as an individual, with the social world around you. As Packer and Goicoechea explain, in their analysis of sociocultural and constructivist theories of learning, while learning 'is considered chiefly in terms of changes in knowing', we should also consider the ways in which it also entails 'broader changes in being' (2000: 227). They recognise that the processes involved in this are by no means straightforward and unproblematic:

> learning involves becoming a member of a community, constructing knowledge at various levels of expertise as a participant, but also taking a stand on the culture of one's community in an effort to take up and overcome the estrangement and division that are consequences of participation. Learning entails transformation both of the person and of the social world.
>
> (2000: 227)

This is a rather more challenging and appropriately problematised notion of the learning that is enabled by, and constructed through, time spent in networked technologies (themselves not the focus of those authors) than the rather more normative conceptions of Jenkins and colleagues. Packer and Goicoechea go on to attribute the key drivers behind such learning to whatever community of practice the potential learners finds themselves in, which can of course also include an online community:

> A community of practice transforms nature into culture; it posits circumscribed practices for its members, possible ways of being human, possible ways to grasp the world – apprehended first with the body, then with tools and symbols – through participation in social practices and in relationship with other people.
>
> (2000: 234)

Thus such learning, as the authors of the MacArthur paper do recognise, is serious and central to the development of individuals as they grapple with the problems and benefits of online participation in the sociocultural sphere. There are excellent reasons, as they suggest, for encouraging formal education to find space within its classrooms for practices such as distributed cognition, multi-tasking, play and networking, within its existing array of pedagogies. Teachers may not be best placed to educate young people in those practices themselves, but if they can do anything to foster and enable the kind of creative and exploratory learning experiences that some of their more enthusiastic technology-using students find for themselves, by taking an interest in what those students know and do, and not getting in the way of their wider sharing even in the classroom, that would be a start.

No-one really knows, though, whether this is all going somewhere. What we have seen so far is that while a very large proportion of teenagers have learnt, quite often teaching one another, to use all sorts of technologies in clever and useful ways, only a small portion of young people seem to have gone further than that. This highly focused sub-section of the teenage population, in many countries round the world, have found for themselves how to weave the distributed knowledge, the networking, negotiations and play of the Internet into their lives in ways that in theory could empower the wider population of their peers, if all equally embraced these modes of experimentation, collaboration and engagement. But just because certain practices associated with these kinds of learning are now taking place on a very large scale indeed, at least within those parts of the world that can afford to be online all the

time, we cannot possibly know yet whether this is fostering new generations of young people who seek, create and share knowledge about their world in transformational ways. Arguably, we should not be leaving it entirely to young people to find out ways of doing these things without the support and interest of the adult world.

Summary

This chapter has looked at the broad picture of whether, and in what ways, young people's learning is enhanced by their access to digital technologies. This was the starting point, indeed, of the research that informs much of the book, and the conclusion to that has been predictably mixed. As we showed in the first part of this chapter, despite over-heated assertions about the educational potential of new technologies in the first flush of the digital era, progress in this respect has turned out to be quite slow and uncertain, constrained in particular by anxieties about the Internet. Nonetheless, very gradually, schools have begun to forge effective ways of using technologies to augment traditional learning, and some aspects of progress – such as the development of online communication between home and school – are encouraging, if not yet fully realised.

In terms of the learning that young people manage for themselves, whether using the Internet for supplementing formal sources of knowledge, supporting each other's homework activities through social networks, or building new skills for the digital era, it is clear that new technologies have been and will continue to be of great importance in their lives. In learning to use those technologies, both in terms of basic technical skills and of more sophisticated digital literacies, young people have proved adept at seeking out new knowledge, sharing their discoveries across the peer group, and finding out how to do the things they want to do. But, despite their capacity to learn on their own and from each other about the technology skills that they perceive as useful, the final message of this chapter is that adults need to engage actively in encouraging and enabling young people to expand the scope and complexity of their digital repertoires.

6 Outliers

Throughout this book we have highlighted the diversity in the ways that teenagers use new technologies and the varying implications this use has in their lives. For the most part we have focused on those young people who are relatively typical in their access, experiences and uses of technology. Yet, contrary to popular opinion not all fit within this mainstream group. Indeed, there are a substantial minority of the teenage population who cannot use new technologies in the ways that their peers take for granted. In this chapter we explore why this is the case and what it really means to be an intermittent user of the Internet and other new technologies. In other words, an 'outlier' compared to the digital mainstream. First we summarise the key 'dimensions of inequality' in uptake of new technologies: access, support networks, skills and confidence and use. Next, in 'Relationship between social and digital exclusion' we consider the extent to which limited or non-existent use of new technologies by young people can be considered some kind of 'digital choice'. Then in Outliers we explore the experiences of three groups of young people: those who do not have sustained Internet access at home, looked after children who experience significant restrictions on their Internet use, and young people with special educational needs who often need significant support to go online. Finally, in 'What are the impacts' we consider the implications of being outside the digital mainstream in both qualitative and quantitative terms.

Dimensions of inequality in uptake of technology

Our understandings of the inequalities in how people access, use and experience new technologies has moved from a notion of a simple dichotomy of digital haves and have-nots to a more complex conceptualisation where there are different and related dimensions of digital inequality, which are continuous in nature and constantly changing

(Chen and Wellman, 2004; van Dijk and Hacker, 2003; van Dijk, 2006). These dimensions relate to issues of access to technology, attitudes towards technology, skills to use technology and the ways in which people use technology. For example, van Dijk provides four kinds of technological access: motivational access, physical access, skills access and usage access (van Dijk and Hacker, 2003). Similarly, DiMaggo and Hargittai (2001) proposed five dimensions of digital inequality: equipment, autonomy of use, skills, social support and purposes of using the Internet (DiMaggo and Hargittai, 2001).

As we have seen in the previous chapters the Internet forms the central focus of most of the activities that young people engage in in relation to technology. Thus, below we review four dimensions of inequality in technology use, with a particular focus on the Internet. Specifically, quality of access, support networks, skills and confidence, and nature of use. As we shall see below, while these four dimensions are typically viewed as sequential, with nature of use as the final outcome (Eynon and Malmberg, 2011a; van Dijk, 2006), they also interrelate and inform one another.

Quality of access

In most developed countries, basic access to the Internet is now widely available, with more and more people being able to access the Internet at home, at school and/or at work (DiMaggo and Hargittai, 2001; Hargittai, 2002; van Dijk, 2006). As basic access is becoming increasingly common the quality of access people have to the Internet becomes more and more important. This is particularly the case for young people, who are nearly all Internet users due to the inclusion of online activities at school.

One typical indicator of quality of access is having the Internet at home. Home Internet access has often been shown to influence the amount and range of activities that young people take up online (Facer *et al.*, 2003; Eynon and Malmberg, 2011b; Ito *et al.*, 2008; Livingstone and Helsper, 2007). Indeed, young people tend to be relatively privileged in developed countries, in that they are the most likely group to have home Internet access (Eynon, 2009; Hughes and Hans, 2001; Ofcom, 2011; Vandenbroeck *et al.*, 2008). As noted in Chapters 3 and 5, this is often because their parents or guardians have made the decision to invest in a computer and Internet connection to support their child's education (Haddon, 2005; Stevenson, 2011).

Yet, a significant minority of young people do not have Internet access at home. For example, in the UK in 2010 14 per cent of young people

aged 8–11 and 11 per cent of young people aged 12–15 did not have home Internet access. Across Europe in 2010, home Internet access rates for households with children varied from 50 per cent in Romania to 99 per cent in the Netherlands and Finland, with 84 per cent the EU average (Eurostat, 2010). In the US in 2010, 12 per cent of young people aged 12–17 did not have home Internet access (Pew, 2011). Not having home Internet access means that young people do not have the opportunities to use the Internet for a wide range of activities, to experiment and play with technology and use the Internet in ways that would benefit them the most (Eynon and Malmberg, 2011b; Ito *et al.*, 2008); and we will return to this issue below.

While home Internet access is perhaps most important, there are other aspects of quality of access that need to be considered when understanding Internet use. For example, the speed, quality of the hardware and software (van Dijk, 2005), the extent to which young people need to share their access with others in the home (Eynon, 2009) and the number of locations of access (Dutton and Blank, 2011; Livingstone and Helsper, 2007). All of these factors related to quality of access are important in understanding the ways that young people use, and benefit from, the use of the Internet and are constantly shifting as technology develops.

Support networks

The level of support a young person has around them is important both in terms of when they first use the Internet and while they are an Internet user (DiMaggo and Hargittai, 2001). This support can come from a range of sources: from the home, from friends, from school or college, from work, and from other institutions such as libraries and Internet cafés.

As we saw in Chapter 3, other family members often influence young people's uses of technology. For example, parents can influence when and how young people are introduced to technology (McMillan and Morrison, 2006), their child's uses of technology once online via the strategies they employ to support and regulate their child's use of technology (Davies, 2011; Tripp, 2010; Valckea *et al.*, 2010; Zhao, 2009), and can act as important role models (Eastin, 2005). Just like wider studies of the relationships between parents and a child's educational outcomes where different levels of parental involvement can have both positive and negative outcomes for their child, a similar process can be seen in the online setting (Eynon and Malmberg, 2011a).

Schools and other educational institutions are also important in this respect, as they may provide an important point of access to the Internet,

and because they can support young people in their development of their digital skills (Eynon and Malmberg, 2011a). However, the level of support young people receive may differ markedly from school to school. For example, a study of schools in the US highlighted that the ways that new technologies were used differed significantly depending on the socio-economic status (SES) of the school catchment area, with those from higher SES using computers in more advanced ways (Warschauer *et al.*, 2004). Yet the relationship between SES and support is complex. For example, a study in the UK demonstrated that schools in higher SES areas tended to give students more support and access to computers outside lessons, but were also more likely to restrict the range of sites students were allowed to use compared to those in lower class areas (Lee, 2008).

In general, friends are a very important source of support in using new technologies, particularly for older teenagers. While more research is required on how this process works, those teenagers who have friends who are more engaged in using technology tend to use the Internet more (Eynon and Malmberg, 2011b; Facer *et al.*, 2001; Ito *et al.*, 2008; Punamäki *et al.*, 2009).

As is clear from above, these support networks are important for understanding how young people use the Internet (Eastin, 2005; Hargittai and Hinnant, 2005; Livingstone and Helsper, 2010; Livingstone *et al.*, 2011). This is for a number of interrelating reasons. First is that the stronger a young person's support network, the more people they have available to ask for help and support when going online. Indeed, research has found that having 'warm experts', that is, having people around that are a little ahead in terms of Internet experience and skills, can be beneficial for uptake and use of technology (Bakardjieva and Smith, 2001, cited in Haddon, 2005). However, it is of course important to consider who these 'warm experts' are and which young people have access to them. If the people around are not that skilled in using the Internet they may not always offer appropriate advice. Indeed, this is supported by a national survey in the US in the mid-nineties that found that teenagers who stopped using the Internet were more likely to be taught by a family member or friend who may not have a lot of expertise in going online (Katz and Aspden, 1998).

The immediacy of support may also be important. Someone who has to seek casual assistance at an Internet café or school may find they cannot solve their problems instantly and this could lead to anxiety or problems that go unresolved. Another important aspect of support in using the Internet is the role of intermediaries or proxy users. That is, people who will use the Internet on behalf of someone else. For young

people who do not have good access to the Internet this may be particularly important and will be considered below.

What is also important to consider here is the relational aspect of Internet use. A teenager's beliefs and perceptions of their online abilities and activities are likely to be influenced by their observations of others around them. The more positive the experiences of parents, friends and teachers in online activities, the more likely the individual is to believe in their own abilities to use or learn to use the Internet (Eastin, 2005). Thus, the people around the individual become good role models for making young people feel confident in their skills and abilities online (Eynon and Malmberg, 2011a). However, this could work both ways if young people feel their skills are not as good as their peers or parents then their online experiences could be negatively affected (Helsper and Eynon, forthcoming). Thus, while the importance of support networks is clear, the effects can be both positive and negative and further work is required to fully understand the dynamic interplay between young people and those around them.

Skills and confidence

The skills young people need to use and benefit from new technologies are complex and multi-faceted. They involve functional skills to operate and use technologies for a range of informational, social and creative purposes (e.g. Ba *et al.*, 2002: 6–8; Eshet-Alkalai and Amichai-Hamburger, 2004: 422–3). They also encompass skills to understand how new technologies influence and are influenced by wider commercial and societal forces (e.g. Buckingham, 2007; Gillen and Barton, 2010; Hague and Williamson, 2009; Jenkins *et al.*, 2007; Livingstone, 2008). Young people vary quite significantly in their level of these skills. For example, a number of studies have highlighted that many young people have relatively low levels of skill to locate, evaluate and use online information (Cranmer *et al.*, 2008; Rowlands *et al.*, 2008; Seiter, 2004).

Skills are important. Numerous studies have shown that those young people with more skills in using the Internet tend to go online for a wider range of activities and benefit more from their time online (Cheong, 2008; Eastin, 2005; Hague and Williamson, 2009; Hargittai and Hinnant, 2008; Helsper and Eynon, 2010; Livingstone and Helsper, 2010). Correspondingly, research with young people in the US has demonstrated that those with the least skills gain the least benefit from using the Internet as they tend not to use it for as wide a range of purposes and are less likely to use the Internet for 'capital enhancing' activities such as informed political participation or using online job search sites to obtain employment (Hargittai and Hinnant, 2008).

However, it is important to stress here that measuring skills is often very difficult, particularly in survey research, which tends to be a popular method for digital inclusion researchers. This is because they are often based on self-report and while someone may think they are good at something (or report they are) this is not the same as actually being good at something (Hargittai, 2005; Hargittai, 2010; Van Deursen and van Dijk, 2009).

That said, the levels of confidence people have in themselves to use new technologies are still relevant. Self-efficacy is extremely important in understanding the extent and in what ways individuals undertake particular tasks or make certain choices (Bandura, 2001). Thus, those that feel more confident or have a higher self-efficacy in using the Internet are more likely to take up online opportunities as they believe there will be a positive outcome for their behaviour (Eastin, 2005). Such a phenomenon does not only relate to the technology, but also to other beliefs that young people hold about themselves. For example, a study of the online information-seeking behaviours of young people demonstrated that self-concept for learning as well as ICT self-efficacy was particularly important for understanding uptake of online information seeking (Eynon and Malmberg, 2011a). This makes sense, because the beliefs young people hold about themselves have implications for educational choices and outcomes (Bong and Skaalvik, 2003). Thus, their beliefs in themselves as learners may influence the likelihood of undertaking certain kinds of activities online.

Indeed, the attitudes people hold about themselves, others and technology play an important part in technology use. For example, a significant amount of research with adults has demonstrated that those who have more positive attitudes towards technology tend to be more likely to use the Internet and use it for a wider range of purposes (Dutton *et al.*, 2007). Similarly, in our study a feeling of having a problem-solving approach to technology (i.e. being able to take control, experiment and play with technology to solve problems) was also important in understanding Internet use (Eynon and Malmberg, 2011b). Broos and Roe (2006) also stress that psychological factors such as computer locus of control are important, and highlight the role of the future goals of adolescents, as these future plans may shape their motivations and expectations of using the Internet (Broos and Roe, 2006). Other work has also explored the role of personality in understanding uptake and usage of the Internet (Hamburger and Ben-Artzi, 2000; McElroy *et al.*, 2007; Ross *et al.*, 2009). Thus, when thinking about dimensions of inequality of technology use, there is a complex interplay between cognitive and social factors.

Nature of use

The online sphere offers a range of opportunities including information seeking (Rieh, 2004), chatting, interacting and communicating (Hew and Hara, 2006; Ross, 2007), and watching videos, listening to music, blogging, sharing pictures, creating content (Rollet *et al.*, 2007); networking and job searching. However, while the vast majority of young people do use the Internet, the ways that they use it are not equal. Young people differ significantly both in the range of activities that they take up online, with some young people tending to take up a far wider range of activities than others (Livingstone and Helper, 2007); and this can be seen as a kind of 'ladder of online opportunities' (Livingstone *et al.*, 2011). Young people differ in the extent to which they use the Internet for social, informational, and entertainment purposes (Peter and Valkenburg, 2006), or other activities (Zillien and Hargittai, 2009). These different uses are likely to lead to different kinds of benefits and challenges and this issue will be discussed further below.

As noted above, nature of use can be seen as a result of the interactions between access, support and skills in using the Internet. To some extent this is true, but use tends to influence these other dimensions too. For example, certain kinds of use may lead to the development of better online skills, connections with new expert others, and/or an interest in purchasing new equipment. These activities will influence quality of access, support and skills that may then lead to uptake of different kinds of online activity.

However, while quality of access, support networks, skills and nature of use are all important there is another very important aspect that underpins all of these relationships – social inequality.

The relationship between digital and social exclusion

Research has shown time and time again that those who are digitally excluded tend, for the most part, to be socially excluded as well. The predominant proportion of young people who do not have Internet access at home are from the lower SES groups, and even when home access is available young people from lower SES homes are less likely to have their own laptop or have the most up-to-date technology. For example, in 2011 in the UK 80 per cent of young people aged 5–15 from lower SES homes had Internet access at home compared to 98 per cent in the highest socio-economic groups (Ofcom, 2012). Similarly, in the US 69 per cent of young people aged 12–17 personally owned a computer in 2010, and this was positively related to household income and age (Pew, 2010).

The number of sources of support an individual has access to is also positively related to income (Dutton and Helsper, 2007), and as we have seen above, schools in higher socio-economic areas tend to give their students a wider range of online experiences in the classroom (Lee, 2008).

Individuals from better-off, better-educated homes tend to benefit more from a wider range of online activities than those from less well-off circumstances (Zillien and Hargittai, 2009). Similarly, Peter and Valkenburg (2006) found that adolescents with lower socio-economic and cognitive resources used the Internet more frequently for entertainment, such as playing online games, than for social or informational purposes. These differences are not just at the general level but at more specific levels too. For example, when we look at information seeking, we see that SES is important in the ways in which young people use the Internet. Young people from higher SES homes in the US (i.e. where their parents had higher levels of education and income) are more likely to seek online information about politics or current events (Lenhart *et al.*, 2010). In the UK SES and uptake of online information-seeking practices for homework are similarly positively related (Eynon and Malmberg, 2011a).

However, the role of SES on uptake of online activities is complex and not necessarily straightforward. For example, Livingstone and Helsper found that SES was indirectly but not directly related to Internet use. In their study SES was relevant in terms of experience (amount of time online) and access to the Internet, which influenced skills and self-efficacy, which in turn influenced uptake of online opportunities (Livingstone and Helsper, 2010). In a study of college students in the US, once number of access locations, laptop ownership and experience was taken into account, the effect of household SES (parental education) was not influential on uptake of online activities (Hargittai, 2010).

Furthermore, a number of studies have recognised the possibility that no or limited use of the Internet may not always be due to social inequality. Research across the whole population in developed countries has shown that there are a group of people who are categorised as being deeply socially excluded but are using the Internet; and the opposite is also true, with others who have all the necessary social resources not going online (Helsper, 2008).

As noted above, the majority of young people in school do use the Internet to some degree, as they have some kind of online access available to them at school. Thus, in contrast to the rest of the population in most developed countries, when we think about those young people outside the digital mainstream it is not in terms of use and non-use so much as low levels or occasional use of the Internet (Livingstone and Helsper, 2007).

Very low or non-existent Internet use among young people may be due to the elements of digital inequality that we have discussed above, but it may also be due to a lack of interest, need or awareness of the benefits it may offer (Livingstone and Helsper, 2007). That is, there may be an element of 'digital choice' by these young people who we may classify as 'outliers' and it may not all be about issues of social exclusion (Haddon, 2004; Wyatt, 2003). While 'choice' is a very difficult concept as it is still shaped within people's existing social structures (Eynon and Helsper, 2011) it is quite useful conceptually as it moves us away from a deficiency model of non-use of the Internet (Selwyn, 2004) or a similar discourse around intermittent use of the Internet by young people.

Internet use is influenced and shaped by other things that are going on in people's lives, their interests, their family and peer networks, their uses of other media and everyday constraints (Haddon, 2005). Furthermore, use of the Internet needs to be considered within a context where other new technologies are being used at the time, thus the impact or meanings of intermittent Internet use may be less important (Selwyn, 2006).

There has been very little research on young people who are outliers, and outside the digital mainstream, probably due to the assumptions many of us hold about young people as the 'net-gens' (Geniets and Eynon, 2011). It is also difficult as the vast majority of research in this area is based on quantitative surveys thus understanding implications are particularly difficult to measure (Livingstone and Helsper, 2007); especially for smaller sub-groups of the population. In the section below we try to begin to open up this discussion by looking at specific instances of 'outliers', with respect in particular to their connections and relationship to the Internet.

The outliers

In this section we shall look at three groups who can be considered outliers in different ways, in essence outside the mainstream or 'on the periphery' of use and experience with the Internet (Murdock, 2002). Each group has particular problems with at least one of the dimensions of digital inequality outlined above. The first group are the disconnected, i.e. those young people who do not have sustained Internet access at home thus have poor quality of access to the Internet. The second group are looked after children who, for important reasons, experience significant restrictions on their Internet use. The third group are young people with special educational needs who often need significant support in terms of their skills and confidence to go online.

The disconnected – young people who do not have Internet access at home

As we saw above, in developed countries, young people are the most likely group to have home Internet access (Eurostat, 2010); and those who do not have the Internet at home are in a minority. Reasons for non-home Internet access are primarily due to cost, and while many more households with young people have Internet access compared to the general population, there are still some families who simply cannot justify the costs of home access to the Internet. Related to this are often parental attitudes and experiences of the Internet:

> My mum doesn't like me going on computers because of the . . . like the MSN and stuff because she don't want me going in chat rooms and stuff, and she thinks it's dangerous.
>
> (Kim, 14)

> My mum's not that keen on the Internet because of things that might like come up when you don't want them too really. And she doesn't really know how to use a computer very much.
>
> (Billy, 15)

In 2010 a quarter of parents across Europe did not use the Internet (Livingstone *et al.*, 2011). Indeed, from our survey in 2009 78 per cent of young people who did not have Internet access at home had parents who did not use the Internet at work. This lack of experience by parents makes it difficult for young people to communicate their interests or need for the Internet at home, or to encourage parents to take the risk and face the fears they may have about their child using the Internet.

> *How sort of keen is your mum?*
> She doesn't like see the point in the Internet.
> *Do they use a computer at all, your parents?*
> My parents, no.
> *Not even at work or something like that?*
> No. My mum's a carer and my dad works in a factory, so they don't really use the Internet.
>
> (Arjan, 14)

This lack of Internet access at home means that young people seek out alternative access locations, such as school, libraries, other family member's or friend's houses (Davies and Spencer, 2010; Ito *et al.*, 2008).

Indeed, for this group of young people, school is often a key access point, the place they were introduced to the Internet, where they develop the skills to go online and a source of support when they encounter difficulties. However, these alternative access locations tend to mean that young people experience a more restricted engagement with the Internet. This is for two main reasons: first, a lack of a convenient connection to the Internet prevents young people from going online as and when they want; second, because many schools and libraries block access to a range of certain sites, such as social networking sites or certain kinds of content.

This limited and restricted access to the Internet has a potentially negative effect on homework, mainly because of the limited amount of time that is available to use a computer and go online.

> We get coursework now in Year 9 to see what groups we're going to go in Year 10 and people with Internet they can get higher marks because they can like research on the Internet. And it's hard for me because I have to like travel [on a bus to the library] and sometimes my mum doesn't let me.
>
> (Arjan, 14)

> I had to write a story about heaven and like I tried to write it in school but it was bell gone and I have a lot of things that I could write and I was angry that I haven't got a computer because I might finish it at home when I've got lots of time to do it. But because when I'm at school I need to do it very fast.
>
> (Sharon, 15)

> I usually find myself having to do the work at school, and it would be a lot better if I could just go home and I could do my work in a quiet environment where there's no one else there . . . so it can get a bit stressful sometimes.
>
> (Billy, 15)

Sometimes, young people in our study reported trying to get others to help support their homework, through a complex set of arrangements. As Josh who didn't have Internet access at home with his mum explains:

> If I have to use the Internet I'll probably end up going to my dad's but he lives in Skegness so it's usually . . . I only get to use the Internet at his every two weeks. Or if I don't see him then I'll ring

him up and ask him to do the work for me. I tell him what he needs to write if, or print out pictures, I'll ask him to do it and send it in the post and he will do that.

(Josh, 14)

Proxy use is often seen across the population of people who do not use or are infrequent users of the Internet. But as this example shows this kind of proxy use is not sufficient or appropriate, particularly when trying to use the Internet to support learning (Eynon, 2009).

Having school as the main point of access to the Internet also means that there is no time to investigate or research areas of personal interest as homework takes priority. Indeed, in our study on the (relatively rare) occasions that young people used the Internet at friends' houses, these more social and informal practices were central.

Sometimes my friend goes on MSN and we talk to like all our friends on there. And sometimes we go on YouTube and stuff like that.
What kind of things do you like on YouTube?
The gymnastics . . . Because I'm interested in gymnastics and I just search for the things I like.

(Kim, 14)

This relates to a desire on the part of many young people in this group to use the Internet like many of their peers, that is, as a way to pass the time, to 'do their own thing' and to not be bored.

I don't really get my one time to do my own little things.

(Alexa, 14)

Sometimes when it's raining [and I can't go out and see my friends] It's really, really boring and I wished I had a computer.

(Sharon, 15)

I'm just like bored at home and I'd rather have Internet to go on.

(Arjan, 14)

The blocking of certain sites is also problematic. For example, at schools in the UK, young people typically cannot access MSN, Facebook and other SNS and chat rooms. A similar context can be found in other countries, such as the US and other parts of Europe.

What can you actually do on these computers?
    On these, nothing. You just work all the time. They've blocked MSN and Facebook, Bebo, MySpace, they've blocked it.

(Arjan, 14)

Blocking of these sites means that young people cannot engage fully with certain social aspects of online interaction, and this has negative implications for their social life. As Ito and colleagues note, based on their large scale study of young people in the US, 'Sporadic, monitored access at schools and libraries may provide sufficient access for basic information seeking, but is insufficient for the immersed kind of social engagements with networked publics that are becoming a baseline for participation on both the interest-driven and the friendship-driven sides [of activity]' (Ito *et al.*, 2008: 36).

For example, one of our participants (Arjan) talked about how he is missing out 'Because my friends are probably on it [MSN] all the day every day. And like they talk about it in school, what happened on MSN'. He also misses out on 'the jokes and stuff online that my friends have' and not being able to 'get hold of them [my friends]'.

Indeed, the differences between how young people use social networking sites that are dependent upon the quality of access is striking. As noted in Chapter 4, in her study of MySpace danah boyd identified a group of young people who did not use MySpace because of a lack of access to the Internet. In our survey in 2009 half of young people aged 12, 14 and 17–19 who did not have home Internet access never used an SNS site compared to 23 per cent of those that did have home access. Similarly, 15 per cent of all young people aged 12, 14 and 17–19 who did not have home Internet access used SNS at least daily compared to 50 per cent of all young people who did have home Internet access.

Thus, young people without Internet access at home do seem to be missing out. We see that a lack of home access is tending to reinforce and compound existing social inequalities for this group, potentially having quite significant consequences for their learning, education and social life, which are felt quite keenly by these young people. For them, being an outlier is not a choice or a statement, but something they have to cope with, and they try as much as possible to fit in with the mainstream despite these challenges.

Looked after children

Looked after children[15] often experience a lack of sustained access to the Internet typically due to the concerns of what and who they may

encounter online, given the very difficult circumstances some of these young people have previously experienced in their lives. In the course of our research, we interviewed some of these young people when they had recently received laptops as part of the Home Access for Targeted Groups (HATG) scheme (see Davies and Spencer, 2010). As we see, issues for these young people are quite different to the disconnected young people above.

These young people did have access to a computer and the Internet at home. They were also carefully supported by their guardians, who structured use of the Internet through setting time limits, helping to find information and discussing the content on the screen. While in some respects this group of young people had better quality of access to the Internet with more support at home than the disconnected young people above, their access was restricted in other ways. In particular via the public location of the computer in the home (e.g. the dining room), the use of tracking systems, and the implementation of strong filtering systems for their home computer, which were linked to or similar to those used by the schools in the local area.

These restrictions meant that this group could do little online that was private and personal to them, use social networking sites or access certain kinds of information unless they could use another machine outside the home and school setting. This led to similar problems to those experienced by the disconnected learners above, feeling left out, causing problems for interacting with their peers and not being able to use the Internet to experiment with their identity or explore future plans in the same way as the digital mainstream can do all the time if they so choose.

Interestingly, in our study, the majority of this group did not strongly object to this level of observation and blocking. This was partly because of the value for their education that they attributed to having access to a home computer and the Internet:

> I understand really because they gave it us for like ... learning purposes, not for fun. Because I've got my GCSEs ... So we use it for that.
>
> (Anna, 15)

Indeed, the ability to do schoolwork at home did lead to benefits echoing the challenges that the disconnected teenagers experienced above.

> Well when it was comes to like homework, because [before] I just had to just really catch up quickly to do everything really quickly.

It did motivate me at the same time, but . . . I was just sort of having a bit of an argument with the school saying you know you can't expect everyone to have a computer or a laptop. And it's like well use your lunch and break time and I was like well I don't . . . when I am supposed to go on my lunch and break?

(Dale, 16)

This more convenient and personalised access also enabled the pursuit of research-led interests, with interviewees describing their online research to support activities such as horse-riding, researching pictures of airplanes and preparing photo collages with pictures on Google images, which sometimes led to related educational benefits at school. Yet, perhaps most significant for this group was simply the act of being given a device and an Internet connection. Looked after children may not have always experienced a very supportive environment. Thus, being given a computer and a connection to the Internet held a very symbolic meaning:

I was never brought up round a computer, my laptop upstairs is the first time I've really used the Internet or any laptop or anything like that [. . .] It was brilliant because . . . I've never had anyone give me anything really . . . to have someone just give me something was like . . . WOW, you know . . . Just that to me means quite a lot to me because that has been given to me and I'm grateful for it . . . I'm cracking on with it.

(Evan, 17)

Thus, just like the disconnected group, looked after children have very similar aspirations for using computers and the Internet for their homework, for their social life and for their own activities that are present among mainstream teenagers. Despite home Internet access coming with conditions and restrictions, this was still something very valuable and important in their lives, perhaps more so in some cases given the difficult life circumstances they had already experienced. Access to a computer and the Internet gave them a chance to improve their future and being given that access at home tells them that others also feel this is possible.

The decisions to place restrictions on the Internet use of these looked after children was the result of careful consideration. There was an understandable desire from policy-makers, practitioners and carers to protect this group from access to inappropriate online content and people that may cause them particular harm given their backgrounds. However,

the lack of privacy and level of filtering was also problematic as it prevented them from developing the necessary skills needed for a full and effective engagement in an online environment (a problem that led one authority we worked with to do away with the restrictions during the course of the programme). Indeed, exposure to and dealing with risk is an important part of growing up (Livingstone *et al.*, 2011). Blanket restrictions do not recognise the important difference between potential risks and actual harms (Livingstone *et al.*, 2011). While these are more difficult to ascertain for this group, it is important to better understand them. Again, this group of outliers are not part of this category through any kind of digital choice.

Young people with Special Educational Needs

Special Educational Needs (SEN) covers a wide range of difficulties and disabilities from minor to severe, all of which make it more difficult for these young people to learn or access education compared to their peers. Young people who fall into this group may have physical, sensory or cognitive disabilities or a combination of all three, and these have different implications for thinking about the quality of access and ability to engage with the Internet (Woodfine *at al.*, 2008).

Given the complexity of factors and diversity of needs and experiences of young people who fall into this group (McKnight and Davies, 2012), we would like to focus here on one aspect. Namely, the important role of support networks for young people in this group. Indeed, this was a significant issue for the group of young people with SEN we spoke to who had recently received laptops as part of the Home Access for Targeted Groups (HATG) scheme (see Davies and Spencer, 2010). Parents and carers of young people with SEN may need to support the people in their care in using the Internet and other new technologies in multiple ways. For example, by helping them to interact productively with the equipment, by monitoring their activities and setting limits, spelling and reading out words, helping to use search terms and downloading music and games onto the computer to keep the children occupied. A key part of this is to try to foster an appropriate level of autonomy and independence:

> . . . you do go on Google and look for things, don't you? If she asks me a question or something, then I'll say: you know, well get your laptop and you can put that in and find the answer yourself. And you do things like that, don't you? Sometimes she gets the spelling

wrong, so we have to help her, so instead of her asking me and me telling her, we make her use the laptop to research it herself and things like that. So hopefully as she gets older and she gets homework from school, she'll know exactly what to do instead of having to keep relying on us to actually get the answers.

(Linda, carer)

While for some young people with SEN total independence is not an achievable goal, the use of a computer and the Internet can (with support from their parents or carers) significantly contribute to their wellbeing. For example, in our study one of our participants, Kat (8 years), was a severely disabled, bed-bound visually impaired girl who was able to do virtually nothing for herself, and her mother had gone to considerable lengths to embed this new machine into the broader framework of provision that she had created for Kat, in partnership with the various professionals supporting her in looking after her daughter.

She can't move around it now, but we'll help her. If you activate something that makes a noise, it's an association net for her, because she knows that she's touched it. And of course, having worked with a similar thing in the past, before she fell really poorly, I absolutely believe that she realises that she's doing it. [. . .] Firework night, we got this set up, and we managed to get it on the web and we were looking for firework displays. We struggled a bit . . . she's always up very late at night, you see . . . and it was so lovely! . . . My boyfriend came in and he managed to set up a big screen, full screen eventually . . . we had all the sounds and everything, it was lovely! It was really good for her, really lovely!

(Sarah, mother)

It is misleading to suggest that technology in itself can be expected to transform the experience and wellbeing of any young person, but this example does show how a tool such as a laptop computer, if adapted to the needs of the user and used in appropriate ways, can be made to achieve benefits that could not easily be achieved otherwise. For many young people with SEN, support networks are very important either in the initial stages of support to independence or as a way to facilitate the benefits of Internet use in collaboration. This puts significant challenges on those adults close to the teenager, which can run from simply knowing how to use a computer in order to support their child that may be common in other families to a greater feeling of responsibility, a particular onus upon them to engage actively in helping their youngsters

to make the most of computers and the Internet for learning and independence.

> Because we've never had a computer, we don't know how to use it
> . . . I'll be looking into doing a computer course . . . so that we can
> have a bit more knowledge.
>
> (Philip's mother)

> And the problem that we've got, this is the first time that we've ever
> come across a computer, so we're a bit computer illiterate.
>
> (Philip's father)

Parents and carers may also need to work with and adapt specialist equipment and software, which can be very complex. Sarah (above) for example acknowledged that a good deal of adaptation on her part has been necessary in order to benefit from the new equipment. She also took care to make clear that she appreciates the provision very much, and understands that personalisation at this level has to be achieved within the home context, with close attention to the specific circumstances and needs of this particular learner.

While it is not possible in this short section to do justice to the range of young people with SEN, it is clear that computers and the Internet can provide an important way for them to become independent and autonomous. In the early stages at least, though, many young people with SEN need to have extra support from those around them to begin to make best use of the Internet in their lives. Thus, in this group some may well become part of the digital mainstream. Yet, for those with more severe difficulties the Internet will always be mediated through the interactions with the significant others around them. Nevertheless, while this group may always be outside the digital mainstream the Internet still has the potential to be an important and significant part of their lives.

What are the impacts?

As has been said many times, today's teenagers have grown up with the Internet. From the cases above, we see that those who fall outside the digital mainstream tend to be there for reasons other than some kind of 'digital choice'. The negative implications for these three groups of young people echo to some extent van Dijk's different types of digital inequality. These types can be grouped into immaterial (life chances, freedom); material (capital resources – economic, social, cultural); social (positions, power, participation); and educational (capabilities and skills) (van Dijk, 2006: 223).

There is some commonality across the three cases. All three groups experienced some kind of restricted access to the Internet. The disconnected group, reliant often on school, encountered problems (in terms of time, location or content available) that influenced their online behaviours and had broader implications for their education and social life (Dresang, 2005; Ito *et al.*, 2008; Lee, 2008). Some similar restrictions (due to home monitoring and filters) were also problematic for the looked after children. For those with SEN challenges can occur when computers are not accessible and usable, which can prevent them from using computers to develop their own sense of agency.

The level of support and the people who support these three groups of teenagers vary quite significantly, and occur for different reasons. For the disconnected learners, they necessarily have to seek support outside the home due to the lack of experience of the Internet their parents are likely to have. The carers of looked after children are significantly more involved due to concerns about their safety, and for young people with SEN that support may be crucial to have any kind of access at all.

These variations in digital inequality lead to different patterns of Internet use, and have quite different implications. The most notable implications for the disconnected group are a feeling of being left out socially, of not being able to do homework properly or as thoroughly as they would like and not being able to simply 'do their own thing' online. The looked after children in our study who had been given home Internet access felt a greater sense of agency and control over their lives and learning, now that they were able to use the Internet for their homework, research their own things and believe in themselves, like the others who had decided they were someone who was 'worth' being given a computer. This is not to say they did not feel frustrated by the lack of privacy in their Internet use and the blocks they encountered on SNS and other important sites, particularly as they got older, but an increase in quality of access had undoubtedly led to some positive experiences for this group. For young people with SEN, the computer and the Internet offered alternative ways to connect with and experience the world, supported by others where needed, but in ways that would hopefully offer them more independence, agency and freedom to achieve their life goals.

While the cases we have looked at are quite small-scale, they do help us to move beyond discussion of Internet use, to a focus on what this use means to individuals. One of the significant problems of a great deal of literature in the area of digital inclusion is that it is quantitative and this makes implications or outcomes of Internet use quite difficult to measure. We need to have a far better understanding of what the Internet

means within the context of people's everyday lives, which acknowledge the socio-cultural dynamics and practices that operate in different ways for different people in different contexts (Mehra *et al.*, 2004; Thomas *et al.*, 2005; Tsatsou, 2011).

In terms of benefits, some quantitative research has found a positive relationship between access to and the use of technologies by school children and educational attainment (Attewell and Battle, 1999; Harrison *et al.*, 2003; Jackson *et al.*, 2006; Papanastasiou *et al.*, 2003). Yet overall, the outcomes have tended to be quite mixed, and the research often suffers from a number of methodological issues (Wittwer and Senkbeil, 2008). Thus, survey data about online activities need to be contextualised in the experiences of people in everyday life (Livingstone and Helsper, 2007; Eynon, 2009). The qualitative cases presented here begin to provide some of these understandings. More work is required, and such qualitative or mixed method studies could be longitudinal in nature to capture longer term impacts, particularly as engagement with the Internet and other new technologies is never linear (Anderson and Stoneman; 2007; 2011; Haddon, 2005; Haythornthwaite and Wellman, 2002; Murdock, 2002; Wyatt *et al.*, 2002).

What is also clear is that the ways these groups need to be properly supported are quite different. In discussing these learners separately from mainstream learners, we are acknowledging that particular effort should be made to ensure that those with exceptional problems or vulnerabilities are strongly included within the education system, especially in terms of wider digital opportunities in the present and in future. Similar to other researchers we argue that there is a need to begin to segment Internet users into better defined groups in order to support them in appropriate ways. One policy will not fit all non-users or users of the Internet (Eynon, 2009).

As an example of this work, some authors have developed typologies of non-Internet users (in the wider population). For example, Wyatt and colleagues put forward four types of non-Internet user: resistors, rejecters, excluded and expelled (Wyatt *et al.*, 2002). Verdegem and Verhoest, found five distinct groups: the 'incapable refusers', those who could afford connections to computers and the Internet, but did not wish to go online – due to limited skills and negative attitudes or a lack of interest; the 'self-conscious indifferents', for whom access and skills tend not to be a barrier but hold negative attitudes towards ICTs or a lack of interest; the 'willing but incapable', for whom skills and access are a problem despite having the motivation and positive attitudes towards going online; the 'skilled ICT lovers with limited access' group, and the 'price-sensitive pragmatists', who have average skills to use ICTs and are

moderately motivated but perceive high barriers to access in terms of cost (Verdegem and Verhoest, 2009: 649). A similar approach could be employed that looked only at young people in particular, that only focused on those outside the digital mainstream. At present such typologies tend to merge such outliers into one group (e.g. Eynon and Malmberg, 2011b).

However, this is less than straightforward as the notion of values needs to be considered alongside concerns about risk. In the UK policy literature, there is perhaps too simplistic a view that use of the Internet is a 'good thing' with more being better (Wyatt, 2003). What is challenging for many researchers in this area is the extent to which we do or should place value on different kinds of activities. Is using the Internet for gaming as important as job seeking? While this seems like an unhelpful question, it may be something that needs to be tackled when trying to support young people online. This is further complicated by the fact that basic uses may lead to more complex (and more valuable) online activities and as online opportunities increase so do does the likelihood of young people encountering risks online (Livingstone *et al.*, 2011). Yet, risks and harms are not the same, as young people may encounter risk online but may not be harmed by it (Livingstone *et al.*, 2011).

Summary

What is clear is that for teenagers, who have grown up surrounded by the Internet, are in the vast majority of cases wanting and expecting to use the Internet to some degree, and despite the hype and rhetoric there are some who still cannot get the necessary level of quality of access and support to use it fully and effectively. Such restrictions do have negative impacts and while we cannot yet quantify these in any clear way, from a qualitative perspective these negative aspects are clear and strongly felt by those young people who find themselves outside the digital mainstream.

7   Autonomy

We have been careful throughout the book to emphasise that young people – specifically, teenagers – can sometimes differ very much from one another in how they use digital technologies, and in the value they attribute to doing so. They are not all enthusiastic users of technology, even if they do mostly take its availability for granted, and feel the absence of it very acutely if denied them. In this final chapter, though, we are not so much concerned with the differences between teenagers in these respects, as with what they have in common in how they experience and perceive digital technologies, and with the extent to which those things are specific or even unique to teenagers.

Out of all the things that might be considered specific to and significant about young people's attraction to technology – its easy fit into youth sub-culture, the vulnerability of young brains, the toy-like nature of digital devices – the one that we suggest here as most worthy of consideration is the notion that digital technologies are important to teenagers because they help them to achieve one of the key goals of adolescence, and something we have alluded to on a number of occasions throughout the book: autonomy. As the textbooks on adolescence make very clear, this reaches right to the heart of the teenage experience:

> Becoming an autonomous person – a self-governing person – is one of the fundamental development tasks of the adolescent years.
> (Steinberg, 2002: 288)

We came across considerable evidence during the course of our own research that digital technologies were particularly valued by teenagers for the ways in which they enable them to do things for themselves, and there was a strong common feeling among them that they needed to have access to technologies in order to be in the main flow of things. We are certainly not in a position to say that extensive time spent online or

using various digital devices really does help young people become autonomous adults more quickly, but this perspective might help us better understand why technology is so important to teenagers as they go through adolescence, both in the value they attribute to it, and in the things it does for them at the time.

In the main section of this chapter, 'Tools for growing up', we explore the ways in which teenagers see technology as important in realising their desire to become more autonomous. In the first two sections we consider how young people try to achieve the various promises of technology associated with growing up, as they move from child to teenager. We go on to look more closely at what it means to seek autonomy as a teenager, and how using technology in support of this works out in practice.

In the 'Conclusion', in addition to bringing together what we see as the key issues relating to autonomy, we also briefly discuss the ways in which young people's experience of technologies in their lives might be expected to stabilise in some respects, and continue to change in others, as we move into the future.

Tools for growing up

Children and technology

Children become aware of the promise of technology from very early on, but this promise only really begins to deliver during the teenage years. For younger teenagers, that mainly involves gaining accelerated access to more grown-up experiences, whereas for older teens technologies are viewed increasingly as instrumental in enabling them to meet quite specific demands of approaching adulthood.

When Apple's iPad first appeared it was described[16] as 'a device whose presence fades away when you use [it]', and perhaps we really are arriving at the long-predicted time when awareness of technology is becoming out-dated, as the things we once thought of as technological become naturalised into daily life, and so easy to use that we no longer notice them as technology. Many toddlers are as familiar now with multi-touch screens as they are with books, and gaining more immediate feedback from them than from any book. But the intensity of engagement and interest displayed by toddlers using iPads does not actually indicate that the allure of something *because* it is technological is about to lose its grip on the consciousness of young people, or that technology will soon cease to be experienced as a distinct category in people's lives.

Hard to fathom as very young children are, we would suggest that from the start they want to play with technologies because they are highly

responsive to their actions, and are therefore both stimulating and entertaining. As they grow older and enter the first years of schooling, children start thinking about technologies as a means of enabling grown-up experiences and freedoms, but – either because of developmental limitations or simply because of a far greater parental regulation – most actually make only limited progress in this respect in the years before adolescence. As we have shown in previous chapters, children begin to make a case for having more technology during the early years of schooling by appealing directly to parents' core anxieties: mobile phones to provide a shield of protection for traversing the threatening spaces between home and school, and computers to ensure educational success. Neither are these entirely artificial concerns on the part of the children: they are made afraid of the outside world, and anxious about being excluded from the perceived digital advantage of their peer group. For most children, technology has both the immediate appeal of a wonderful toy, and the amorphous necessity of life insurance: they don't wish to find themselves exposed one day by the lack of it. They feel this as much as their parents do.

It takes some time, in younger children's experience, for the satisfactions of possessing technology to begin to match its desirability. For many the fun element fails to deliver very much, the safety factor turns out to be a mixed blessing in terms of constant parental oversight, and the educational relevance of using technology, during the first years of schooling at least, seems to consist of little more than learning to use technology. In terms of the young people we interviewed, it appeared that in their pre-teen years only a relatively small proportion found the digital world to be a particularly engaging or fulfilling place where learning, socialising, and having digital fun actually engaged them for any length of time. For rather more children of pre-teen ages, it seemed that technology turned out mainly to offer some promise of keeping boredom at bay for a while.

As we suggested in Chapter 2, the pre-teen years serve above all as a necessary apprenticeship to the practices, rules and etiquettes of digital networked technologies. It was only as they began to move through the teenage years that they began to find some substance in what they wanted to make technology do for them, either singly or, more often, along with their peers.

Teenagers and technology

Many younger teenagers we spoke to had by this stage in their adolescence come to view digital technologies as their control centre for

achieving the various short-term and long-term goals of their lives, exploiting all the resources of their laptops and phones:

> You can pretty much get all of the things on there. You can get like TV, you can get books like Book Clicks on the Internet. And you can get like media, like BBC iPlayer and ITV stuff. So that's the one I'd choose for just like those reasons because it's all rolled into one. And you've got like your talking, you've got your phone, you've got everything on there really.
>
> (Lucy, 13)

Kathy, below, surrounded herself with the various technology resources she needed, to insure herself against the threat of ever being cut off from entertainment, from the company of friends, and from the whole buzz of the digital universe, while Ashley expressed a feeling of technology enabling him to be an active agent in his life:

> Sometimes I will do some collages or editing pictures, because I absolutely love messing around on the computer . . . normally when I get on the computer there is about ninety something people online, and I probably talk to about twenty of them . . . my phone goes everywhere with me, I'm not joking. I take it with me when I go to the bath. I cannot go anywhere without my phone, even if I go downstairs to get a drink I take my phone with me.
>
> (Kathy, 14)[17]

> I use [the computer] for my like music, phone, as well as the actual just *doing* stuff on it. Whereas with the telly I only watch it . . .
>
> (Ashley, 15)

As teenagers move through the mid-teenage years, they come increasingly to value the instrumental as well as the symbolic qualities of technology; something that reliably enables them to take actions they need to take, leaving behind the more trivial preoccupations of a few years earlier: 'when I was like thirteen then it would be the bee's knees to have a PlayStation. But now it's just sort of like another thing cluttering up my desk' (Stu, 15). For teenagers growing up, technology is seen not merely as a way of passing the time, but also as a dynamic resource that allows them to act upon their world:

> With Internet I can get more in depth and like get higher results on my own, my GCSE work.
>
> (Arjan, 15)

Paula is an archetypal mid-teens technology user; a model of the mainstream teenager. She told us she uses her mobile phone in order to text her friends throughout the day, and tended to spend more time using technology during her weekday evenings than during her weekends (a very typical practice in our experience, suggesting that adult anxieties about youngsters never going out because they are stuck in front of a screen have limited basis in reality: the teenagers we spoke to were mostly determined to get out of the house as a matter of course at weekends). She was hoping to have a career in journalism, which stemmed from her love of English lessons at school, and reading gossip magazines. She was not yet clear about how to get into this, but she knew that she wanted to write about people's lives, and that this would be a job she would enjoy. She said, when pressed, that technology would be quite important for this career as 'I think I'll have to like look online and write up online and stuff'. Her main hobby involved writing short stories on the computer, for her friends and her sister. She sends chapters over MSN to her friends, and these tend to be love stories, but she only writes these when 'life inspires me'.

Technology did not appear to be a big deal for Paula, in the sense that she thought about it or liked to talk about it very much, but the ability to choose it and use it clearly afforded her a sense of self-direction, of agency, in being able to do all the different things that mattered to her by way of entertainment, creativity, sociability, and working towards her future. On the surface, that is more or less how most adults regard technology also, but there is one major difference between adults and teenagers in this respect: the degree of freedom they experience in choosing what to do, and how to do it, in their lives. It is the job of teenagers to extend the boundaries of their freedoms beyond what parents consider desirable, and by the time they are teenagers they have come to consider that digital technologies afford them multiple means of acting independently of parental control. This puts their technology use right at the heart of key issues of adolescence such as independence, agency and autonomy.

Perspectives on autonomy

Autonomy is not the exclusive concern of teenagers. Steinberg points out that the desire for autonomy is a major goal throughout life, beginning with toddlers, and carrying right on into old age. But it is certainly the case that adolescence provides a powerful combination of drivers, in terms of biological, cognitive and social changes (2002: 289), which do mean that the teenage urge for autonomy is particularly intense; and

complex. Indeed, as Zimmer-Gembeck and Collins suggest, it is possible to identify a number of distinct dimensions of autonomy during adolescence, such as: behavioural ('active independent functioning including self-governance'), cognitive ('a sense of self-reliance, a belief that one has control over his or her own life') and emotional ('a sense of individuation from parents and relinquishing dependence on them') (2003: 176).

This is not to suggest that the desire for autonomy means that all adolescents are simply going flat-out to escape from parental control: adolescents quite reasonably want increased freedom within a context of reliable protection and, as Smetana claims (see Chapter 3), conflict with parents is not the norm. Most value the safety and comforts of home, during a period in which the majority of them are emotionally and economically dependent on their parents, and in seeking individuation from parents are not necessarily seeking detachment (Zimmer-Gembeck and Collins, 2003: 180). According to Steinberg, autonomy should not be confused with rebellion – 'adolescents fare best when their relationships at home strike the right balance between autonomy and connectedness' (2002: 295).

Technology is very well-suited to providing certain experiences of freedom, without actually removing young people from the protection of the home. It is very easy to show many instances where technology provides safely bounded experiences of autonomous action (e.g. seeking information about future study or employment for oneself online), providing simulated experiences of control, (for instance when playing games), and engendering experiences of individuation (developing an identity over Facebook). It is far from easy to say, though, whether or not this is a positive aspect of technology use: do virtual experiences provide a helpful foundation for difficult real-world interactions, or are they rather a light-weight substitute for the real thing?

Possibly the first of these to make an impact in young people's lives is the way in which technologies enable young people to experience control long before they enter adolescence, by playing video games. These constitute the first and most rewarding experiences of using technology for many children, offering both satisfying feedback to their own actions and providing (for instance in the case of NeoPets) strong experiences of emotional engagement. James Paul Gee describes this as the 'amplification of input principle' (Gee, 2003: 64) whereby games give a lot of output for a little input. As they grow older, keen game players begin to discover increasingly rich experiences of the impact of their own decisions, sometimes experiencing god-like mastery and control over the pseudo-presences within virtual worlds and electronic games-play:

> I'm more of a kind of person that likes to command sort of big armies of people into battle, kind of thing . . . because I'm like a megalomaniac you know . . . I like the sort of power, the being able say like, you go there and them actually doing it and the sort of control, I guess.
>
> (Craig, 14)

> It's [The Sims] just like you can like express yourself and like be creative and stuff, and you can kill everybody . . . You know, it sounds like the finale when you kill everyone it's like . . . oh. And you can just make people foresee their own lives and like make different choices and stuff and I like that sort of thing.
>
> (Lucy, 13)

Shaffer argues that the most important thing about technology is that it lets us work with 'simulations of the world around us' which 'let us play with reality by creating imaginary worlds where we can do things that we otherwise couldn't do at all' (2006: 9). Both Shaffer and Gee are primarily concerned with the positive kinds of learning that they argue are stimulated and structured by game-play, but we should not disregard the more fundamental outcomes of playing games, which involve the psychological benefits of enhanced self-efficacy beliefs, a sense of flow, and the experience of mastery. Interestingly, whether knowingly or otherwise, parents are possibly contributing to the development of their children's future autonomy as adults by allowing them the opportunities, often from early on in their lives, to engage with the simulated challenges of games. Rathunde, writing in the context of Csikszentmihalyi's theories of flow, argues that the uniquely (compared with other primates) extended period of human children's dependency on adults leads to a productive relationship between independence and autonomy, including 'an increase in play behaviour (freedom at the moment), resulting in turn in a more elaborate development of the cerebral cortex and greater adult freedom and flexibility' (1988: 361). Rathunde was not thinking specifically of computer games, but the relevance seems striking here, if we can see computer game play as a substitute for the challenges of the outside world, which takes place in a safe environment where certain kinds of neurological growth might take place. At the very least, such a hypothesis provides an interesting counterpoint to the rather more alarming perspectives from neuroscience that Susan Greenfield (see Chapter 2) has proposed, in which the development of pathways in children's brains might in some ways become damaged by over-engagement in onscreen experiences.

Of course, parents tend to feel quite antagonistic to video games and excessive social networking, seeing them as a distraction from more traditional notions of childhood and growing up, and just bad for children ('apparently when I've been on MSN for a while I get quite aggressive and tired and stuff'; Ellie, 15). But research is beginning to offer more upbeat interpretations of this particular tension:

> Society's traditional adolescent issues – intimacy, sexuality, and identity – have all been transferred to and transformed by the electronic stage. Among the hallmarks of the transformation are greater teen autonomy, the decline of face-to-face communication, enhancement of peer group relations at the possible expense of family relations, and greater teen choice. Given the connectedness between the physical and virtual worlds, the challenge is to keep adolescents safe (both physically and psychologically) while at the same time allowing for the explorations and interactions that are crucial for healthy psychosocial development.
>
> (Subrahmanyam and Greenfield, 2008: 139–40)

Such more balanced viewpoints on teenage technology use are even finding their way into the media, even if the popular stereotypes of teenagers will not be so easily erased.

TEENAGE SOCIAL MEDIA BUTTERFLIES
MAY NOT BE SUCH A BAD IDEA

Kids most likely to spend a lot of time texting and on Facebook, among other networking sites, may be more well-adjusted, studies suggest.

With his gaze fixed on a tiny screen, hearing plugged by earbuds and fingers flying, the average teenager may look like a disaster in the making: socially stunted, terminally distracted and looking for trouble. But look beyond the dizzying array of beeping, buzzing devices and the incessant multi-tasking, say psychologists, and today's digital kids may not be such a disaster after all. Far from hampering adolescents' social skills or putting them in harm's way, as many parents have feared, electronics appear to be the path by which children today develop emotional bonds, their own identities, and an ability to communicate and work with others.[18]

Even so, despite quite high levels of awareness among teenagers themselves of adult concerns about the Internet and excessive time spent in front of a screen, it is part of the parental role to attempt to moderate

and regulate their children's behaviour and for the most part teenagers are not antagonistic to their parents' concern for their wellbeing. And of course the measures that young people have to take in order to accommodate or work round parental objections constitute further fertile opportunity for the development of independent decision-making and agency.

The development of teenagers' cognitive autonomy, going beyond the satisfying experiences of control that begin with game play, can be observed in the way that they begin to feel increasingly able to apply the technology tools available to them to study and follow personal interests as they grow older. It is possible to detect a clear sense of self-efficacy in 15-year-old Debbie's concluding comment to her account (quoted in Chapter 2) of what happens when friends ask her to edit out their blotchy skin in photos: 'so I do.' Samuel says something quite similar in concluding the story of how he set up his own computer at home:

> it just came to me once, and I thought – because I watched the movies and like they have the dual screens with the – you know – FBI and all sorts, and just working on loads of screens. And I just thought, 'I could do that!'

> (Samuel, 15)

According to Zimmer-Gembeck and Collins, 'autonomy requires a sense of agency', which is to say 'operating from one's core sense of self . . . self-initiating and self-regulating' (2003: 182). Young people, alone with a computer, can choose to act out a wide range of self-initiated and self-regulated actions, and whether these occur in the simulated environments of games, or in online environments where their actions may impact upon other live humans, the actor him or herself may feel an equally strong sense of agency, either by killing off a Sims character, competing with someone during a multiplayer game, or placing a home-made video on YouTube. In these respects, the very uncertain distinction between the virtual and real world is likely to be less important than the force of the experience that the user can construct with the help of technology. Zimmer-Gembeck and Collins' comment that 'individuals construct the ability to regulate one's own cognitions, emotions, and behaviour from a history of transactions with the environment. Individuals must engage in self-regulatory practices to develop autonomous functioning' (2003: 183) could perhaps be extended to apply to the learning of self-regulated practices that arguably occurs in the course of a young person's ongoing partnership with their computer over time. We would suggest that cognitive autonomy development related to technology use

ultimately occurs holistically, as teenagers become increasingly adept at using their own particular repertoire of technologies.

While the development of cognitive autonomy relates mainly to the largely individualistic notion of agency, the third aspect of autonomy development – emotional – depends primarily on the opportunities teenagers experience to connect and form co-operative relationships with other people, especially their peers. Such connectedness and co-operation is also, of course, fundamental to teenagers' experience of digital technologies, through chat, social networking, online game playing and other forms of online co-operation, arguably contributing to the 'positive psychological development' that, according to Steinberg, enables teenagers to learn 'to function both independently and interdependently'. He concludes that:

> These dual goals – what some writers have called agency (acting autonomously) and communion (connecting with others) . . . define the psychosocial agenda during adolescence.
>
> (Steinberg, 2002: 314)

Hegelson makes a very clear distinction between these two aspects of positive psychological development: 'Agency reflects one's existence as an individual, and communion reflects the participation of the individual in a larger organism of which the individual is a part.' Her particular account of these aspects of personal behaviour acknowledges problematic aspects with each, which she sees as corresponding strongly to male vs. female gender roles in modern US society at least, so that either orientation un-moderated by the other can on occasions lead to unhealthy or unhappy states. But she also shows that in general communion is associated with beneficial outcomes such as social self-esteem and support (Hegelson, 1994: 415).

Despite the emphasis on notions of collaboration and co-constructed experiences online that has surrounded discussion of the Internet (especially in socio-cultural discourses), researchers (including ourselves) tend to be quite tentative when it comes to asking young people to reveal private information about their lives, and there is a consequent lack of qualitative evidence especially about some of teenagers' personal and intimate interactions online. But such explorations are a significant aspect of adolescents' activity online. Subrahmanyam and Greenfield suggest that the Internet offers important opportunities for instance to sexual minority adolescents, as 'a safe haven for sexual exploration without the prejudice and harassment that gay, lesbian, and bisexual adolescents sometimes face at the hands of peers and adults' (2008: 129),

and of course sexual majority adolescents also benefit from the opportunity provided by their online affiliations to explore issues that very many find difficult to discuss with parents. Subrahmanyam *et al.* point to several studies that show that teens seek 'information about sexuality and relationships with great frequency', even if 'Up until now, adolescents' peer conversations about sex and sexuality were hard to study' (2006: 396). Their own study casts useful light on young people's sexual expression in chat rooms, but is not able (given the nature of inter-actions studied) to offer any evidence of any more mutually supportive kinds of interactions online between teenagers regarding emotional or sexual issues that may quite possibly occur in the more socially structured contexts of social networking sites.

We did catch a number of glimpses, though, of some of the ways in which teenagers can provide a mutual support network online, sometimes for straightforwardly practical purposes, such as developing online networking skills –

And where did you get that advice to do that from? [. . .] It's just all our friends do it, because generally one friend helps another set something up, and then there's like a chain so the one who has already set one up will just pass on the information.

(Claire 15)

– or sometimes for issues touching on the participants' personal lives and social relations. Liam below is clearly proud of the quality of support and mutual respect that he and his friends had established with their online interactions:

What do I talk about? Um, just talk about school, talk about relationships, talk about like private stuff really, just stuff between friends, stuff between friends and just have fun really. Don't really talk about anything . . . We just worked it out, yeah. It's mainly through politeness, it's mainly through manners and everything, which causes us to do it that way.

(Liam, 15)

That is not to ignore the negative interactions that do most definitely occur between teenagers online, which we discussed in Chapter 3. As we said then, it is not always easy to distinguish between real bullying, which certainly takes place online, engagement in online dramas, and the kind of teasing interactions that teenagers are quite used to in their daily relations with one another. Facebook, in particular, has created its

own set of dilemmas and users have to figure out new forms of etiquette for dealing with the online break-up.[19] All of these can lead to problems that sometimes drive teenagers away from online social interactions altogether. It is the higher visibility of these typical teenage issues that causes concern, among both adults and some teenagers, but perhaps instead of viewing these as new kinds of problem, it might equally be the case that this visibility ultimately offers rich opportunities for young people to confront and deal with complex interpersonal issues, with quite positive implications for the development of emotional autonomy. The evidence in these respects is very limited still, whereas uninformed guesswork on the topic (in the form especially of websites aimed at parents, and horror stories in the popular press) is widely available.

Summary

It is possible to identify a wide number of ways in which teenagers benefit from digital technologies as they work through the various struggles and excitements of growing up. The evidence and insights touched on throughout the present chapter, and indeed during the whole of this book, at the very least support what has been said many times before: digital technologies are highly important in the lives of young people. On the basis of the accumulated perspectives and evidence we have presented here, we would go further and say that the ways in which teenagers involve new technologies in their lives turn out to be of substantial value to them in their processes of seeking autonomy and growing up. Whatever the drawbacks and problems associated with teenage technology use, young people have nonetheless evolved ways of adapting the tools of technology to their own desires and needs that merit serious attention and some degree of respect from the adult world.

The key question here is whether or not these uses of technology go beyond being straightforward exploitation of useful tools for doing what they would have done anyway, and begin to constitute a newly evolved process of growing up. Our argument here has little to do with the digital native notion of a generalised affinity with technologies among young people. Rather, we would say that teenagers have a developmental inclination to seek independence and autonomy, individually and through peer group affiliations, and this inclination in particular is what drives them to make the effort to seek, improvise and share practices of using technology that, however flawed in some respects, appear to help them towards the goals of growing up. Most importantly, we do argue that this constitutes a change, a new element of growing up that did not exist prior to the invention of the personal computer, the Internet and the mobile phone.

In Chapter 3 we concluded that the digital world does not actually constitute an additional *context* in young people's lives, but that it does constitute a significant additional *element* – one that has to be bought and paid for. That expense carries with it a notable contradiction in terms of issues of growing up and autonomy: for the most part, young people get to use or possess digital technologies through negotiation with parents, on whom they are increasingly economically dependent to an extent that is somewhat at odds with actual autonomy. But, as perspectives on learning through play suggest (as proposed by Rathunde above), the tension between autonomy and dependency is potentially a very productive aspect of growing up. The explorations of adult behaviour and independent decision-making that occur online are in different respects both real and unreal. They have real implications, in that relationships, conflicts and desires explored online are very often worked out at the same time in the offline world, and unreal aspects in that some of these experiences are no more than simulations of the real world – but simulations, nonetheless, whereby skills and understandings can be developed in relatively safe contexts.

Young people, as we have remarked a number of times, would not anyway wish to be deprived of their technologies. Nor, of course, would they wish to be deprived of TVs or junk food, so that does not prove much, admittedly. But we believe that the things they say about what these technologies mean to them, as they go through the process of growing up, signifies in the end a wholly different level of importance in their lives from any other medium, or any other kind of treat.

Closing

Throughout this book we have sought to represent as faithfully as possible the understandings about teenagers and their technology lives that emerged from what young people told us during the course of our own research. The picture that we found illuminated a great deal about how technology blends in with the family life, friendships, aspirations and concerns of adolescents. We were constantly impressed by the thoughtfulness and generosity of these young people, in telling us about themselves and the things they did. It is impossible to pull together all of those things in these final words, but in coming to an end we would like to consider the following perspectives at least:

1   Teenagers choose from much the same range of technologies as adults, but are strongly influenced in what they do with these by the shared and distributed practices of the peer group; to that extent, it is reasonable to contend that there is such a thing as a specifically teenage technology sub-culture.
2   Teenagers align themselves to these technology practices and this sub-culture in widely varying ways: some embracing them whole-sale, others engaging in them rather more selectively, and a small number frustrated by their lack of opportunity to use them at all.
3   We believe that the technology practices and sub-culture of teenagers can play a valuable role in helping them cope with the experiences of adolescence and the transition towards adulthood. We recognise also, though, that a case can be made for seeing them also as a worrying distraction from the serious demands of education, and as unmediated access to the worst aspects of the adult world.

This is not an evergreen set of issues that have been worked through in each previous teenage generation, but rather the consequence of the rapid and – to adults at any rate – bewildering formation of new

opportunities, problems and conditions surrounding adolescence. It is hard to know what to do for the best. If teenagers have their own unique sub-culture of technology, how can adults expect to penetrate that deeply enough to help their children deal with it? If teenagers really vary so much in the importance they attribute to these things, how can adults judge whether to push them to explore further, or pull them back? And if the teenage world of technology is such a mixture of the positive and the negative, how on earth do adults help teenagers make the right choices?

Actually, of course, the importance of technology in teenagers' lives is not really so hard to fathom, even if the discourses and preoccupations that can be found there will always be somewhat mysterious to adults. But it is easy enough to grasp the central appeal of these things to teenagers: they see technologies as shifting the balance of things in their favour, just a bit. Protected and supported as most teenagers may be, they also feel frustrated by the relatively small amount of power and control they have in their lives, as adolescents in the parental home, as pupils in school, and as individuals in the highly pressured social world of the peer group. In all these respects, technologies are seen as enabling them to exercise increased choice in how they pass the time, present a viable self-identity, have visibility and respect in the crowd, and exercise control in meeting the demands of study that have been imposed upon them. The cultural aspect of this can be found most of all in the knowledge and values shared between them about what to do with technologies and how to do these things, but each teenager also has to make their own decisions about how far they want to take that.

This was particularly evident in the way that Facebook washed across the whole picture during the years in which our research was carried out. By the time of our final conversations with the teenagers in our study, it was evident that no-one could ignore the pressure within the peer group to belong and to participate constantly. For some this meant taking the difficult decision of preferring not to join in, but for most it involved commitment to an increased intensity of engagement with their peer group, with all the excitements, conflicts and dramas entailed. Insofar as Facebook aspires to embody and bring together the whole of its users' online lives in the future, some would argue that it increasingly threatens to limit the scope of those very opportunities it purports to make available. These ambitions extend now to Facebook becoming the platform for the mobile devices that will become central in young people's technology lives over the next few years.

Maybe Facebook will brilliantly realise these ambitions, and equally it may gradually fade from view, to be replaced by something, or many

things, that are subtly or substantially different. Perhaps Twitter represents more closely the model of the next stage of online culture for young and old alike, in terms of an exponential growth in fast, loosely structured and free-flowing conversations and content shared across cyberspace. A version of this notion is interestingly proposed by Jennifer Egan, in scenes set in a near-future New York at the end of her novel *A Visit to the Goon Squad*. Egan envisages a ubiquitous technology in the form of a 'handset' owned by every adult, and child, used for everything (including, especially, the marketing and consumption of popular culture and goods), and woven into all communication, far or near. Conversation has become multimodal and multilayered, blending the evolved sharpness of what Egan calls 'T' (i.e. text) messages into the vocal conversation of two people in the same room (Egan, 2011: 329):

> Lulu T'd: *Nvr met my dad. Dyd b4 I ws brn.* Alex read this one in silence. 'Wow. I'm sorry,' he said, looking up at Lulu, but his voice seemed too loud – a coarse intrusion . . . He managed to T: *sad . . . Ancnt hstry,* Lulu T'd back.

This raises the credible prospect of a step-shift in how people might come to talk to one another in the near future, in which the back channel of texts and tweets – an innovation with a short history but a major impact – has evolved into a kind of parallel co-channel of human intercourse. Whether or not something of that kind would ever emerge, the point is that the opportunities and challenges that all of us face as technologies develop will require us to make decisions about how far, and for what purposes, we want to go along with the functionalities and attractions we are offered.

Increasingly, children are drawn from early on into new forms of communication, interaction and engagement in the good and less good aspects of the adult world by opportunities to use technologies, certainly long before they reach adolescence. These are challenges that adults need to engage with, we suggest: although it is clear that teenagers can always be expected to find their own routes through these things, they also deserve some support, interest and even guidance from adults in doing so. This is not merely because we must warn them off serious negative aspects, but also – more so, we suggest – because without adult help, they cannot be expected to discover the scope and richness of the world of social interaction and shared knowledge that technology opens up for them.

Notes

1 http://blog.hubspot.com/blog/tabid/6307/bid/5263/Do-You-Have-Digital-Natives-at-Your-Organization.aspx (accessed 12 October 2011).

2 Keynote at Oxford Internet Institute conference *A Decade in Internet Time*, at Saïd Business School, Oxford, 22 September 2011

3 **JULIET**
How camest thou hither, tell me, and wherefore?
The orchard walls are high and hard to climb,
And the place death, considering who thou art,
If any of my kinsmen find thee here.
ROMEO
With love's light wings did I o'er-perch these walls;
For stony limits cannot hold love out . . . (Shakespeare, W. *Romeo and Juliet.*
Act II scene ii)

4 http://byod.hanoverpublic.org/byod-policy (downloaded 13 February 2012).

5 www.olweus.org/public/bullying.page.

6 'We look at the present through a rear-view mirror, we march backwards into the future', McLuhan and Fiore (1967) *The Medium is the Massage.*

7 http://en.wikipedia.org/wiki/Vannevar_Bush (downloaded 8 November 2011).

8 http://en.wikipedia.org/wiki/Memex (downloaded 8 November 2011).

9 www.paleofuture.com/blog/2007/9/20/classroom-of-the-future-part-1-1987.html (downloaded 8 November 2011).

10 www.paleofuture.com/blog/2007/4/19/connections-atts-vision-of-the-future-part-7-1993.html (downloaded 8 November 2011).

11 www.youtube.com/watch?v=ZIA2g_PIfJ8 (downloaded 9 November 2011).

12 www.pil-network.com/resources/tools (accessed 23 April 2012).

13 It seems rather more encouraging and appropriate that Microsoft is joining up with other tech giants to encourage the teaching of computer coding in schools www.bbc.co.uk/news/technology-15916677 (accessed 28 November 2011).

14 'Social networking has revolutionized the way that we interact with those around us, and educational networking is here to revolutionize our classrooms. Rather than networking focused on sharing personal photos and the latest scoop, educational networks provides teachers with a new way to facilitate collaboration among their students, and share in their learning experiences' (http://calgaryscienceschool.blogspot.com/2011/11/edmodo-social-networking-designed-by.html?utm_source=feedburner&utm_medium=feed&utm_campaign=Feed:+blogspot/ybHY+%28Connect%29; downloaded 7 December 2011).

15 The term 'looked-after children' is the term in the UK used to describe young people who are looked after by the state in accordance with the relevant national legislation. They may be placed with family, extended family/friends or foster carers.

16 www.macworld.com/article/1150424/ipad.html (accessed 18 April 2012).

17 Feeling a bit stranded used to be considered a part of adolescence, and one that developed inner resources. Now it is something that the network makes it possible to bypass. Teenagers say that they want to keep their cell phones close, and once it is with you, you can always 'find someone' (Turkle, 2010: 243).

   This is a new non-negotiable: to feel safe, you have to be connected (Turkle, 2010: 247).

18 http://articles.latimes.com/2010/may/18/science/la-sci-socially-connected-kids-20100518 (downloaded 11 April 2012).

19 See www.nytimes.com/2011/08/07/magazine/teaching-kids-how-to-break-up-nicely.html?_r=2&smid=tw-nytmag&seid=auto.

Bibliography

Aarsand, P. (2007) Computer and video games in family life: the digital divide as a resource in intergenerational interactions. *Childhood*, 14, 235–58.

Adams, G. R. and Berzonsky, M. (2003) *Blackwell Handbook of Adolescence*. London: Blackwell.

Alsaker, F. D. and Kroger, J. (2006) Self-concept, self-esteem and identity. In S. Jackson and L. Goossens (eds), *Handbook of Adolescent Development*. London: Psychology Press, 90–117.

Anderson, B. and Stoneman, P. (2007) Predicting the socio-technical future (and other myths). Chimera Working Paper 2007–10, Colchester: University of Essex, UK.

Anderson, B. and Stoneman, P. (2011) Net gains: the returns to education of home Internet access. Paper presented at the iCS-OII 2011 symposium 'A Decade in Internet Time', 21–23 September, University of Oxford, Oxford, UK.

Ardley, N. (1981) *World of Tomorrow*. London: Etc.

Arthur, W. B. (2009) *The Nature of Technology: What it is and How it Evolves*. London: Allen Lane.

Attewell, P. and Battle, J. (1999) Home computers and school performance. *The Information Society*, 15(1), 1–10.

Ba, H., Tally, W. and Tsikalas, K. (2002) Investigating children's emerging digital literacies. *Journal of Technology, Learning and Assessment*, 1(4): 1–49.

Bandura, A. (2001) Social cognitive theory: an agentic perspective. *Annual Review of Psychology*, 52, 1–26.

Bauman, Z. (1998) *Globalization: The Human Consequences*. New York: Columbia University Press.

Becta (2003a) *What the Research Says About Network Technologies in Teaching and Learning*. Coventry: Becta.

Becta (2003b) *What the Research Says About ICT and Motivation*. Coventry: Becta.

Bennett, S., Maton, K. and Kervin, L. (2008) The 'digital natives' debate: a critical review of the evidence. *British Journal of Educational Technology*, 39(5), 775–86.

Biesta, G. and Tedder, M. (2007) Agency and learning in the lifecourse: towards an ecological perspective. *Studies in the Education of Adults*, 39(2), 132–49.

Bong, M. and Skaalvik, E. (2003) Academic self-concept and self-efficacy: how different are they really? *Educational Psychology Review*, 15(1), 1–39.

Boulton, D. and Hammersley, M. (1996) Analysis of unstructured data. In R. Sapsford and V. Jupp (eds), *Data Collection and Analysis*. London: Sage, 282–97.

boyd, d. (2007) Why youth (heart) social network sites: the role of networked publics in teenage social life. In D. Buckingham (ed.), *Youth Identity and Digital Media*. Cambridge, MA: MIT Press, 119–42.

Brannen, J. and O'Brien, M. (1995) Childhood and the sociological gaze: paradigms and paradoxes. *Sociology*, 29, 729–37.

Broos, A. and Roe, K. (2006) The digital divide in the playstation generation: self-efficacy, locus of control and ICT adoption among adolescents. *Poetics*, 34: 306–17.

Brown, C., Czerniewicz, L. and Pedersen, J. (2008) Doing it for themselves: how South African students learn to use computers for their studies. Paper presented at the 10th Annual Conference of WWW Applications. 3–5 September, Cape Town, South Africa.

Buckingham, D. (1998) Review essay: children of the electronic age? Digital media and the new generational rhetoric. *European Journal of Communication*, 13(4), 557–65.

Buckingham, D. (2001) New media literacies: informal learning, digital technologies and education. In J. Hallgarten, L. Ross and D. Tambini (eds), *A Digitally Driven Curriculum*? London: IPPR.

Buckingham, D. (2007) Digital media literacies: rethinking media education in the age of the Internet. *Research in Comparative and International Education*, 2(1), 43–55.

Buckingham, D. (ed.) (2008) *Youth Identity and Digital Media*. Cambridge, MA: MIT Press.

Burnett, R. and Marshall, P.D. (2003) *Web Theory: An Introduction*. London: Routledge.

Byron, T. (2008) Safer children in a digital world: the report of the Byron Review. London: Department for Education (DfE).

Caldwell, J.T. (2000) Introduction: theorizing the digital land rush. In J.T. Caldwell (ed.), *Theories of the New Media. A Historical Perspective*. London: The Athlone Press, 1–35.

Castells, M. (2011) A decade in Internet time. Paper presented at the Oxford Internet Institute, 22 September, University of Oxford, Oxford, UK. Available online at: www.oii.ox.ac.uk/events/?id=451 (accessed 1 May 2012).

Chen, W. and Wellman, B. (2004) The global digital divide: within and between countries. *IT and Society*, 1(7), 39–45.

Cheong, P.H. (2008) The young and the techless? Investigating Internet use and problem-solving behaviors of young adults in Singapore. *New Media and Society*, 10(5), 771–91.

Christensen, P. and Prout, A. (2005) Anthropological and sociological perspectives on the study of children. In S.M. Greene and D.M. Hogan (eds), *Researching Children's Experiences: Approaches and Methods*. London: Sage, 42–61.

Coleman, J. (2008) Theories of youth development: controversies of age and stage. Paper presented at the ESRC seminar series: 'The educational and social impact of new technologies on young people', 12 March, University of Oxford, Oxford, UK. Available online at: www.education.ox.ac.uk/wordpress/wp-content/uploads/2010/07/Seminar-1-Report.pdf (accessed 1 May 2012).

Coleman J.C. (2011) *The Nature of Adolescence.* 4th edn. London: Routledge.

Coles, B. (1995) *Youth and Social Policy.* London: UCL Press.

Corsaro, W.A. (2004) *The Sociology of Childhood.* Thousand Oaks, CA: Pine Forge Press.

Cranmer, S., Potter, J. and Selwyn, N. (2008) *Learners and Technology: 7–11 Final Report.* Becta: Coventry.

Crockett, L.J. (1997) Cultural, historical and subcultural contexts of adolescence: implications for health and development. *Faculty Publications, Department of Psychology.* Paper 244. Available online at: http://digitalcommons.unl.edu/psychfacpub/244 (accessed 1 May 2012).

Cuban, L. (1993) Computers meet classroom: classroom wins. *Teachers College Record,* 95(2), 185–210.

Davies, J. (2012) Facework on Facebook as a new literacy practice. *Computers and Education,* 59(1), 19–29.

Davies, C. (2010) *The Learner and their Context: Synthesis of Overall Project Findings and Recommendations.* Oxford: Department of Education, University of Oxford.

Davies, C. (2011) Digitally strategic: how young people respond to parental views about the use of technology for learning in the home. *Journal of Computer Assisted Learning,* 27(4), 324–35.

Davies, C. and Spencer, D. (2010) *Narrowing Gaps and Supporting the Vulnerable.* Oxford: Department of Education, University of Oxford.

Dearnley, J. and Feather, J. (2001) *The Wired World: An Introduction to the Theory and Practice of the Information Society.* London: Library Association Publishing.

van Dijk, J.A. (2005). *The Deepening Divide: Inequality in the Information Society.* London: Sage.

van Dijk, J.A. (2006) Digital divide research, achievements and shortcomings. *Poetics,* 34, 221–35.

van Dijk, J.A. and Hacker, K. (2003). The digital divide as a complex and dynamic phenomenon. *The Information Society,* 19, 315–26.

DiMaggio, P. and Hargittai, E. (2001) *From the 'Digital Divide' to 'Digital Inequality': Studying Internet Use as Penetration Increases.* Princeton, NJ: Center for Arts and Cultural Policy Studies, Princeton University.

DfEE (Department for Education and Employment). (1997) *Connecting the Learning Society, National Grid for Learning,* London: Department for Education and Employment.

Dresang, E.T. (2005) The information-seeking behavior of youth in the digital environment. *Library Trends,* 54(2), 178–96.

Dutton, W.H. and Blank, G. (2011) *The 2011 OxIS Survey. The Internet in Britain.* Oxford: Oxford Internet Institute, University of Oxford.

Dutton, W.H. (1996) Introduction. In W.H. Dutton (ed.), *Information and Communication Technologies: Visions and Realities*. Oxford: Oxford University Press, 1–17.

Dutton, W.H. and Helsper, E. (2007) *The 2007 OxIS Survey. The Internet in Britain*. Oxford: Oxford Internet Institute, University of Oxford.

Dutton, W.H., Shepherd, A. and di Gennaro, C. (2007) Digital divides and choices reconfiguring access: national and cross-national patterns of Internet diffusion and use. In B. Anderson and M. Brynin (eds), *Information and Communications Technologies in Society: E-living in a Digital Europe*. London: Routledge, 31–46.

Eastin, M. (2005) Teen Internet use: relating social perceptions and cognitive models to behavior. *Cyberpsychology and Behavior*, 8(1), 62–75.

Eastin, M.S. and LaRose, R. (2000) Internet self-efficacy and the psychology of the digital divide. *Journal of Computer-Mediated Communication*, 6. Available online at: www.ascusc.org/jcmc/vol6/issue1/eastin.html (accessed 1 March 2009).

Egan, J. (2011) *A Visit from the Goon Squad*. London: Corsair.

Ellingson, L. (2009) *Engaging Crystallization in Qualitative Research*. Thousand Oaks, CA: Sage.

Erikson, E. (1963) *Identity: Youth and Crisis*. New York: W.W. Norton.

Erstad, O., Gilje, O., Sefton-Green., J. and Vasbø, K. (2009) Exploring 'learning lives': community, identity, literacy and meaning. *Literacy*, 43(2) 100–106.

Eshet Alkali, Y. and Amichai-Hamburger, Y. (2004) Experiments in digital literacy. *CyberPsychology and Behavior*, 7(4), 421–9.

Eurostat (2010) 80% of young Internet users in the EU27 active on social media. Eurostat news release. Available online at: http://epp.eurostat.ec.europa.eu/cache/ITY_PUBLIC/4–14122010-BP/EN/4–14122010-BP-EN.PDF (accessed 1 May 2012).

Eynon, R. (2009) Harnessing technology: the learner and their context. How young people use technologies outside formal education. Survey report. Coventry: Becta.

Eynon, R. (2009) Mapping the digital divide in Britain: implications for learning and education. *Learning, Media and Technology*, 34 (4), 277–90.

Eynon, R. and Helsper, E.J. (2011) Adults learning online: digital choice and/or digital exclusion? *New Media and Society*, 13(4), 534–51.

Eynon, R. and Malmberg L. (2011a) Understanding the online information seeking behaviours of young people: the role of networks of support. *Journal of Computer Assisted Learning*. Available online at: http://onlinelibrary.wiley.com/doi/10.1111/j.1365–2729.2011.00460.x (accessed 2 January 2012).

Eynon R. and Malmberg, L. (2011b) A typology of young people's Internet use: implications for education. *Computers and Education*, 56, 585–95.

Facer, K. and Furlong, R. (2001) Beyond the myth of the 'cyberkid': young people at the margins of the information revolution. *Journal of Youth Studies*, 4(4), 451–69.

Facer, K., Furlong, J., Furlong, R. and Sutherland, R. (2001) What's the point of using computers? The development of young people's computer expertise in the home. *New Media and Society*, 3(2), 199–219.

Facer, K., Furlong, J., Furlong, R. and Sutherland, R. (2003) *Screenplay: Children and Computing in the Home*. London: Routledge Falmer.

Fielding, M. (2001) Students as radical agents of change. *Journal of Educational Change*, 2(2), 123–41.

Fine, G.A. (2004) Adolescence as cultural toolkit: high school debate and the repertoires of childhood and adulthood. *The Sociological Quarterly*, 45(1), 1–20.

Flew, T. (2002) *New Media: An Introduction*. Oxford: Oxford University Press.

Friesen, N. (2009) *Re-Thinking E-Learning Research: Foundations, Methods and Practices*. New York: Peter Lang.

Furlong, J. and Cranmer, C. (2009) Beyond 'student voice' researching young people's digital learning lives: some intellectual and methodological challenges. Paper presented at the BERA Conference, 3–5 September, University of Manchester, Manchester, UK.

Furlong, J. and Davies, C. (2012) Young people, new technologies and learning at home: taking context seriously. *Oxford Review of Education*, 38(1), 45–62.

Gabriel, T. and Richtel, M. (2011) Inflating the software report card. *New York Times*. Available online at: www.nytimes.com/2011/10/09/technology/a-classroom-software-boom-but-mixed-results-despite-the-hype.html?_r=1&pagewanted=1 (accessed 7 December 2012).

Gates, B. (1985) *The Road Ahead*. London: Viking Penguin.

Gee, J.P. (2003) *What Video Games Have To Teach Us About Learning and Literacy*. Basingstoke: Palgrave Macmillan.

Geniets, A. and Eynon, R. (2011) Breaking out or breaking off? Discontinued Internet use of young people in the UK: a literature review. Draft process document for the Nominet Trust. Available online at: www.nominettrust.org.uk/knowledge-centre/articles/breaking-out-or-breaking (accessed 1 May 2012).

Gershon, I. (2010) Media Ideologies: An Introduction. *Journal of Linguistic Anthropology*, 20(2), 283–93.

Giddens, A. (1990) *The Consequences of Modernity*. Cambridge: Polity Press.

Giddens, A. (1991) *Modernity and Self-identity: Self and Society in the Late Modern Age*. Cambridge: Polity Press.

Gillen, J. and Barton, D. (2010) *Digital Literacies. Research briefing for the TLRP-TEL (Teaching and Learning Research Programme – Technology Enhanced Learning)*. London: London Knowledge Lab, Institute of Education.

Goffman, E. (1959) *The Presentation of Self in Everyday Life*. New York: Anchor.

Goode, J. (2010) The digital identity divide: how technology knowledge impacts college students. *New Media and Society*, 12(3), 497–513.

Graber, J.A., Brooks-Gunn, J. and Petersen, A.C. (1996) *Transitions Through Adolescence: Interpersonal Domains and Context*. Mahwah, NJ: Erlbaum.

Green, E. and Singleton, C. (2009) Mobile connections: an exploration of the place of mobile phones in friendship relations. *The Sociological Review*, 57(1) 125–44.

Greene, S. and Hill, M. (2005) Researching children's experiences: methods and methodological issues. In S. Greene and D. Hogan (eds), *Researching Children's Experiences: Approaches and Methods*. London: Sage, 1–22.

Greenfield, S. (2009) How Facebook addiction is damaging children's brains. A leading neuroscientists chilling warning. *Daily Mail*. Available online at: www. dailymail.co.uk/femail/article-1172690/How-Facebook-addiction-damaging-childs-brain-A-leading-neuroscientists-chilling-warning.html#ixzz1UQfz0w4p (accessed 13 October 2011).

Greenhow, C. and Robelia, E. (2009a) Old communication, new literacies: social network sites as social learning resources. *Journal of Computer-mediated Communication*, 14(4), 1130–61.

Greenhow, C. and Robelia, E. (2009b) Informal learning and identity formation in online social networks. *Learning, Media and Technology*, 34(2), 119–40.

Haddon, L. (2000) Social exclusion and information and communication technologies. Lessons from studies of single parents and the young elderly. *New Media and Society*, 2(4), 387–406.

Haddon, L. (2004) *Information and Communication Technologies in Everyday Life: A Concise Introduction and Research Guide*. Oxford: Berg.

Haddon, L. (2005) Personal information culture: the contribution of research on ICTs in everyday life. Paper for the conference UNESCO between Two Phases of the World Summit on the Information Society?, May 17–20, St. Petersburg, Russia.

Hague, C. and Williamson, B. (2009) *Digital Participation, Digital Literacy, and School Subjects. A Review of the Policies, Literature and Evidence*. Bristol: Futurelab.

Hamburger, Y.A. and Ben-Artzi, E. (2000). The relationship between extraversion and neuroticism and the different uses of the Internet. *Computers in Human Behaviour*, 16(4), 441–9.

Hargittai, E. (2002) Second-level digital divide: differences in people's online skills. *First Monday*, 7(4).

Hargittai, E. (2005). Survey measures of web-oriented digital literacy. *Social Science Computer Review*, 23(3), 371–9.

Hargittai, E. and Hinnant, A. (2008) Digital inequality? Differences in young adults use of the Internet. *Communication Research*, 35(5), 602–21.

Harrison, C., Comber, C., Fisher, T., Haw, K., Lewin, C. and Lunzer, E. (2003) *ImpaCT2 the Impact of Information and Communication Technologies On Pupil Learning and Attainment*. Coventry: BECTA.

Helgeson, V.S. (1994). Relation of agency and communion to well-being: evidence and potential explanations. *Psychological Bulletin*, 116, 412–28.

Helsper, E.J. (2008) *Digital Inclusion: An Analysis of Social Disadvantage and the Information Society*. London: Communities and Local Government.

Helsper, E.J. and Eynon, R. (2010) Digital natives: where is the evidence? *British Educational Research Journal*, 36(3), 503–20.

Helsper. E.J. and Eynon, R. (forthcoming) Distinct skill pathways to digital engagement. Submitted to the *European Journal of Communication*.

Hembrooke, H. and Gay, G. (2003) The laptop and the lecture: the effects of multitasking in learning environments. *Journal of Computing in Higher Education*, 15(1), 46–64.

Henley, J. (2010) Teenagers and technology: 'I'd rather give up my kidney than my phone'. *The Guardian*. Available online at: www.guardian.co.uk/lifeand style/2010/jul/16/teenagers-mobiles-facebook-social-networking (accessed 23 December 2011).

Hew, K. and Hara, N. (2006). Identifying factors that encourage and hinder knowledge sharing in a longstanding online community of practice. *Journal of Interactive Online Learning*, 5(3), 297–317.

Hogan, B. (2010) The presentation of self in the age of social media: distinguishing performances and exhibitions online. *Bulletin of Science, Technology and Society*, 30(6), 377–86.

Holland, D., Lachicotte, W., Skinner, D. and Cain, C. (1998) *Identity and Agency in Cultural Worlds*. Cambridge, MA: Harvard University Press.

Holloway, S.L. and Valentine, G. (2000) Spatiality and the new social studies of childhood. *Sociology*, 34, 763–83.

van House, N.A. (2009) Collocated photosharing, story-telling and the performance of self. *International Journal of Human-Computer Studies,* 67, 1073–86.

Hughes, R. and Hans, J.D. (2001) Computers, the Internet, and families: a review of the role new technology plays in family life. *Journal of Family Issues*, 22(6), 776–90.

Illeris, K. (2003) Learning, identity and self-orientation in youth. *Young*, 11(4), 357–76.

Ito, M., Horst, H., Bittanti, M., boyd, d., Herr-Stephenson, B., Lange, P.G., Pascoe, C.J. and Robinson, L. (with Baumer, S., Cody, R., Mahendran, D., Martínez, K., Perkel, D., Sims, C. and Tripp, L.) (2008) *Living and Learning with New Media: Summary of Findings from the Digital Youth Project*. The John D. and Catherine T. MacArthur Foundation Reports on Digital Media and Learning.

Ito, M., Baumer, S., Bittanti, M., boyd, d., Cody, R., Herr-Stephenson, B., Horst, H., Lange, P.G., Mahendran, D., Martinez, K., Pascoe, C.J., Perkel, D., Robinson, L., Sims, C. and Tripp, L. (2010) *Hanging Out, Messing Around, and Geeking Out*. Cambridge, MA: The MIT Press.

Jackson, L., von Eye, A., Biocca, F., Barbatsis, G., Zhao, Y., and Fitzgerald, H. (2006) Does home Internet use influence the academic performance of low-income children? *Developmental Psychology*, 42(3), 429–35.

James, A. and Prout, A. (1997) *Constructing and Reconstructing Childhood: Contemporary Issues in the Sociological Study of Childhood*. London: Falmer Press.

James, A., Jenks, C. and Prout, A. (1998) *Theorising Childhood*. Cambridge: Polity Press.

Jenkins, H., Clinton, K., Purushotma, R., Robison A.J. and Weigel, M. (2006) *Confronting the Challenges of Participatory Culture: Media Education for the 21st Century*. The MacArthur Foundation.

Jones, C. (2011) Students, the net generation and digital natives: accounting for educational change. In M. Thomas (ed.), *Deconstructing Digital Natives: Young People, Technology, and the New Literacies*. Abingdon: Routledge, 30–48.

Jones, C. (2012) Networked Learning and digital technology. Paper presented at the 11th International Conference on Networked Learning, April 2012, Maastricht, Netherlands.

Jones, C. and Ramanau, R. (2009) The Net Generation entering university: The experiences of first year students. Paper presented at CAL 2009, March 23–25 Brighton, UK.

Jung, J.Y., Qiu, J.L. and Kim, Y.C. (2001) Internet connectedness and inequality – beyond the 'divide'. *Communication Research*, 28(4), 507–35.

Katz, J. and Aspden P. (1998) Internet dropouts in the USA. *Telecommunications Policy*, 22(4–5), 327–29.

Kay, A. (1991) Computers, networks and education. *Scientific American Magazine*. Special issue on communications, computers, and networks. Available online at: www.vpri.org/pdf/sci_amer_article.pdf (accessed 26 April 2012).

Kennedy, G., Judd, T., Churchward, A., Gray, K. and Krause, K. (2008) First year students' experiences with technology: are they really digital natives? *Australasian Journal of Educational Technology*, 24(1), 108–22.

Kling, R. (2000) Learning about information technologies and social change: the contribution of social informatics. *The Information Society*, 16, 217–32.

Kosareff, S. (2005) *Window to the Future*. San Francisco, CA: Chronicle Books.

Kroger, J. (1996) *Identity in Adolescence: The Balance between Self and Other*. London: Routledge.

LaMaster, J. and Stager, G.S. (2012) Point/counterpoint: should students use their own devices in the classroom? *Learning and Leading with Technology*, 39(5).

LaRose, R., Mastro, D. and Eastin, M.S. (2001) Understanding Internet usage – a social-cognitive approach to uses and gratifications. *Social Science Computer Review*, 19(4), 395–413.

Larson, R.W. (2002) Globalisation, societal change and new technologies. What they mean for the future of adolescence. In R.W. Larson, B.B. Brown and J.T. Mortimer (eds), *Adolescents' Preparation for the Future: Perils and Promise – A Report of the Study Group on Adolescence in the 21st Century*. London. Blackwell, 1–31.

Leander, K.M., Phillips, N.C. and Headrick Taylor, K.H. (2010) The changing social spaces of learning: mapping new mobilities. *Review of Research in Education*, 34(1), 329–94.

Lee, L. (2008) The impact of young people's internet use on class boundaries and life trajectories. S*ociology*, 42, 137–52.

Lenhart, A. Ling, R., Campbell, S. and Purcell, K. (2010) *Teens and Mobile Phones*. Pew Internet and American Life Project. Available online at: http://pew internet.org/Reports/2010/Teens-and-Mobile-Phones.aspx (accessed 1 March 2011).

Lenhart, A., Purcell, K., Smith, A. and Zickuhr, K. (2010) *Social Media and Young Adults*. Pew Internet and American Life Project. Available online at: www.pewinternet.org/Reports/2010/Social-Media-and-Young-Adults.aspx (accessed 1 March 2011).

Lewis, C. and Fabos, B. (2005) Instant messaging, literacies, and social identities. *Reading Research Quarterly*, 40(4), 470–501.

Livingstone, Sonia and Bober, Magdalena (2004) *UK Children Go Online: Surveying the Experiences of Young People and their Parents*. London: London School of Economics and Political Science.

Livingstone, S. (2007). From family television to bedroom culture: young people's media at home. In E. Devereux (ed.), *Media Studies: Key Issues and Debates*. Thousand Oaks, CA: Sage, 302–21.

Livingstone, S. (2008) Taking risky opportunities in youthful content creation: teenagers' use of social networking sites for intimacy, privacy and self-expression. *New Media and Society,* 10(3), 393–411.

Livingstone, S. (2009). *Children and the Internet: Great Expectations and Challenging Realities*. Cambridge: Polity Press.

Livingstone, S. and Helsper, E.J. (2007) Gradations in digital inclusion: children, young people and the digital divide. *New Media and Society*, 9(4), 671–96.

Livingstone, S. and Helsper, E.J. (2008) Parental mediation of children's Internet use. *Journal of Broadcasting and Electronic Media*, 52, 581–99.

Livingstone, S. and Helsper, E.J. (2010) Balancing opportunities and risks in teenagers' use of the Internet: the role of online skills and Internet self-efficacy. *New Media and Society*, 12(2), 309–29.

Livingstone, S., Haddon, L., Görzig, A. and Ólafsson, K. (2011) *Risks and Safety on the Internet: The Perspective of European Children. Full Findings*. London: EU Kids Online, LSE.

Packer, M.J. and Goicoechea, J. (2000) Sociocultural and constructivist theories of learning: ontology, not just epistemology. *Educational Psychologist*, 35(4), 227–41.

MacKenzie, D. and Wajcman, J. (1985) Introductory essay: the social shaping of technology. In D. MacKenzie and J. Wajcman (eds), *The Social Shaping of Technology*. Milton Keynes: Open University Press, 2–26.

Marcia, J.E. (1966) Development and validation of ego identity status. *Journal of Personality and Social Psychology*, 3, 551–8.

Martin, D.B. (2000) *Mathematics Success and Failure among African-American Youth: The Roles of Sociohistorical Context, Community Forces, School Influence, and Individual Agency*. Mahwah, NJ: Lawrence Erlbaum.

Marwick, A.E. and boyd, d. (2011) I tweet honestly, I tweet passionately: Twitter users, context collapse, and the imagined audience. *New Media and Society*, 13(1), 114–33.

Matthews, S. (2007) A window on the 'new' sociology of childhood. *Sociology Compass,* 1(1), 322–34.

Mayer-Schönberger, V. (2009) *Delete – The Virtue of Forgetting in the Digital Age*. Princeton, NJ: Princeton University Press.

McElroy, J., Hendrickson, A., Townsend, A. and DeMarie, S. (2007) Dispositional factors in Internet use: personality versus cognitive style. *MIS Quarterly*, 31 (4), 809–820.

McKay, S., Thurlow, C. and Toomey Zimmerman, H. (2005) Wired whizzes or techno slaves? Teens and their emergent communication technologies. In A. Williams and C. Thurlow (eds), *Talking Adolescence: Perspectives on Communication in the Teenage Years*. New York: Peter Lang, 185–203.

McLuhan, M. and Fiore Q. (1967) *The Medium is the Massage*. London: Penguin Books.

McMillan, S. and Morrison, M. (2006) Coming of age with the Internet: a qualitative exploration of how the Internet has become an integral part of young people's lives. *New Media and Society*, 8(1), 73–95.

McKnight, L. and Davies, C. (2012) The Kellogg College Centre for Research into Assistive Learning Technologies. *Journal of Assistive Technologies*, 6(2).

Mehra, B., Merkel, C. and Peterson-Bishop, A. (2004) The Internet for empowerment of minority and marginalized users. *New Media and Society*, 6(6), 781–802.

Merchant, G. (2012) Unravelling the social network: theory and research. *Learning, Media and Technology*, 37(1), 4–19.

Miles, M. and Huberman, M. (1994) *Qualitative Data Analysis: An Expanded Sourcebook*. Thousand Oaks, CA: Sage.

Murdock, G. (2002) Tackling the digital divide: evidence and intervention. Paper given to The Digital Divide Day Seminar, 19 February, British Educational Communications and Technology Agency, Coventry, UK.

Nach, H. and Lejeune, A. (2010) Coping with information technology challenges to identity: a theoretical framework. *Computers in Human Behavior*, 26, 618–29.

Nasman, E. (1994) Individualisation and institutionalisation of childhood in today's Europe. In J. Qvortrup, M. Bardy, M. Sgritta and H. Wintersberger (eds), *Childhood Matters: Social Theory, Practice and Politics*. Aldershot: Avebury, 234–48.

Nathanson, A.I. (1999) Identifying and explaining the relationship between parental mediation and children's aggression. *Communication Research*, 26(2), 124–43.

Nathanson, A.I. (2001) Parent and child perspectives on the presence and meaning of parental television mediation. *Journal of Broadcasting & Electronic Media*, 45, 201–20.

NGfL (National Grid for Learning). (2002) *Transforming the Way We Learn – A Vision for the Future of ICT in Schools*. London: Department for Education and Skills, London.

Norris, P. (2001) *Digital Divide? Civic Engagement, Information Poverty and the Internet Worldwide*. Cambridge: Cambridge University Press.

Ofcom (2010a) UK children's media literacy. London: Ofcom. Available online at: http://stakeholders.ofcom.org.uk/binaries/research/media-literacy/ukchildren sml1.pdf (accessed 1 May 2012).

Ofcom (2010b) The consumer's digital day: a research report by Ofcom and GFK. London: Ofcom. Available online at: http://stakeholders.ofcom.org.uk/binaries/research/811898/consumers-digital-day.pdf (accessed 17 October 2011).

Ofcom (2011) UK children's media literacy report. London: Ofcom. Available online at: http://stakeholders.ofcom.org.uk/binaries/research/media-literacy/media-lit11/childrens.pdf (accessed 1 May 2012).

Ofcom (2012) Media lives summary report 2011 – wave 7. London: Ofcom. Available online at: http://stakeholders.ofcom.org.uk/binaries/research/media-literacy/media-lives.pdf (accessed 1 May 2012).

Oliver, M. (2012) Learning with technology as coordinated sociomaterial practice: digital literacies as a site of praxiological study. Paper presented at the 11th International Conference on Networked Learning, April 2012, Maastricht, Netherlands.

Osgerby, B. (2004). *Youth Media*. London: Routledge.

Papert, S. (1982) Tomorrow's Classrooms? *Times Educational Supplement*, 5 March, pp. 31–2.

Packer, M.J. and Goicoechea, J. (2000) Sociocultural and constructivist theories of learning: ontology, not just epistemology. *Educational Psychologist*, 35(4), 227–41.

Papanastasiou, E., Zembylas, M. and Vrasidas C. (2003) Can computer use hurt science achievement? The USA results from PISA. *Journal of Science Education and Technology*, 12(3), 325–32.

Parry, J. (2006) The transitions to adulthood of young people with multiple disadvantages. In C. Leccardi and E. Ruspini (eds), *A New Youth? Young People, Generations and Family Life*. Aldershot: Ashgate, 276–98.

Peter, J. and Valkenburg, P. (2006) Adolescents' Internet use: testing the 'disappearing digital divide' versus the 'emerging digital differentiation' approach. *Poetics*, 34: 293–305.

Pew (2011) *Generations 2011*. Pew Internet Surveys.

Prensky, M. (2001) Digital natives, digital immigrants: part 1. *On the Horizon*, 9(5), 1–6.

Preston, P. (2001) *Reshaping Communications*. London: Sage.

Punamäki, R., Walleniusa, M., Hölttöa, H., Nygårdc, C.-H. and Rimpeläc, A. (2009) The associations between information and communication technology (ICT) and peer and parent relations in early adolescence. *International Journal of Behavioral Development*, 33(6), 556–64.

Rathunde, K. (1988) Optimal experience and the family context. In M. Csikszentmihalyi and S.I. Csikszentmihalyi (eds), *Optimal Experience – Psychological Studies of Flow in Consciousness*. Cambridge: Cambridge University Press.

Richardson, L. (2000) Writing: a method of inquiry. In N.K. Denzin and Y.S. Lincoln (eds), *Handbook of Qualitative Research*. Thousand Oaks, CA: Sage.

Richtel, M. (2011) A Silicon Valley school that doesn't compute. *New York Times*. Available online at: www.nytimes.com/2011/10/23/technology/at-waldorf-school-in-silicon-valley-technology-can-wait.html?_r=3&hp=&pagewanted=all (accessed 24 November 2011).

Rieh, S. (2004) On the web at home: information seeking and web searching in the home environment. *Journal of the American Society for Information Science and Technology*, 55(8), 743–54.

Robins, K. and Webster, F. (1999) *Times of the Technoculture: From the Information Society to Virtual Life*. London: Routledge.

Rollett, H. Lux, M., Strohmaier, M., Dösinger, G. and Tochtermann, K. (2007). The web 2.0 way of learning with technologies. *International Journal of Learning Technology*, 3(1), 87–107.

Ross, C., Orr, E.S., Sisic, M., Arseneault, J.M., Simmering, M.G. and Orr, R.R. (2009) Personality and motivations associated with Facebook use. *Computers in Human Behavior*, 25(2), 578–586.

Rowlands, I., Nicholas, D., Williams, P., Huntington, P., Fieldhouse, M., Gunter, B., Withey, R., Jamali, H., Dobrowolski T. and Tenopir, C. (2008) The Google generation: the information behaviour of the researcher of the future. *Aslib Proceedings*, 60 (4), 290–310.

Rudduck, J. (2006) The past, the papers and the project. *Educational Review*, 58(2), 131–43.

Savage, J. (2007) *Teenage: The Creation of Youth Culture*. London: Viking Books.

Seiter, E. (2004) The Internet playground. In J. Goldstein, D. Buckingham and G. Brougere (eds), *Toys, Games and Media*. Mahwah, NJ: Erlbaum, 93–109.

Selwyn, N. (2003) 'Doing IT for the kids': re-examining children, computers and the 'Information society'. *Media, Culture and Society*, 25(3), 351–78.

Selwyn, N. (2004) Reconsidering political and popular understandings of the digital divide. *New Media and Society*, 6(3), 341–62.

Selwyn, N. (2004) Exploring the role of children in adults' adoption and use of computers. *Information Technology and People*, 17(1), 53–70.

Selwyn, N. (2006) Digital division or digital decision? A study of non-users of computers. *Poetics*, 34, 273–92.

Selwyn, N. (2008) Realising the potential of new technology? Assessing the legacy of New Labour's ICT agenda 1997–2007. *Oxford Review of Education*, 34(6), 701–702.

Selwyn, N. (2011) *Education and Technology. Key Issues and Debates*. London: Continuum.

Selwyn, N. (2012) Making sense of young people, education and digital technology: the role of sociological theory. *Oxford Review of Education*, 38(1), 81–96.

Sengupta, S. (2011) Online learning, personalized. *New York Times*. Available online at: www.nytimes.com/2011/12/05/technology/khan-academy-blends-its-youtube-approach-with-classrooms.html?_r=1 (accessed 7 December 2011).

Sfard, A. and Prusak, A. (2005) Telling identities: in search of an analytic tool for investigating learning as a culturally shaped activity. *Educational Researcher*, 34(4), 14–22.

Shaffer, D. (2006). *How Computer Games Help Children Learn*. New York: Palgrave Macmillan.

Sidoli, N.C (2011) Early history of computers: machines for mass calculation. Presentation at Waseda University, SILS, Science, Technology and Society (LE202). Available online at: www.aoni.waseda.jp/sidoli/STS_Intro_07.pdf (accessed 2 November 2011).

Silverstone, R., Hirsch, E. and Morely, D. (1992) Information and communication technologies and the moral economy of the household. In R. Silverstone and E. Hirsch (eds), *Consuming Technologies: Media and Information in Domestic Spaces*. London: Routledge, 15–32.

Smetana, J. G. (2011) *Adolescents, Families, and Social Development: How Teens Construct their Worlds*. Chichester: Wiley-Blackwell.

Spencer-Oatey, H. (2007) Theories of identity and the analysis of face. *Journal of Pragmatics*, 39(4), 639–56.

Steinberg, L. (2002) *Adolescence*. New York: McGraw-Hill.

Steinkuehler, C. (2008) Cognition and literacy in massively multiplayer online games. In D. Leu, J. Coiro, C. Lankshear and K. Knobel (eds), *Handbook of Research on New Literacies*, Mahwah, NJ: Erlbaum, 611–34.

Stevenson, O. (2011) From public policy to family practices: researching the everyday realities of families' technology use at home. *Journal of Computer Assisted Learning*, 27(4) 336–46.

Stonier, T. and Conlin, C. (1985) *The Three Cs: Children, Computers and Communication*. Chichester: John Wiley and Son.

Stryker, S and Burke, PJ (2000) The past, present, and future of an identity. *Social Psychology Quarterly*, 63(4), 284–97.

Subrahmanyam, K. and Greenfield, P. (2008) Online communication and adolescent relationships. *Children and Electronic Media*, 18(1) 119–46.

Subrahmanyam, K., Smahel, D. and Greenfield, P. (2006) Connecting developmental constructions to the Internet: identity presentation and sexual exploration in online teen chat rooms. *Developmental Psychology*, 42(3), 395–406.

Takahashi, T. (2010) MySpace or Mixi? Japanese engagement with SNS (social networking sites) in the global age. *New Media and Society*, 12(2), 453–75.

Tapscott, D. (1997) *Growing Up Digital: The Rise of the Net Generation*. New York: McGraw-Hill.

Tapscott, D. (2009) *Grown Up Digital: How the Net Generation is Changing Your World*. New York: McGraw-Hill.

Thomas, F. Haddon, L., Gilligan, R. Heinzmann, P. and de Gournay, C. (2005). Cultural factors shaping the experience of ICTs: an exploratory review. In L. Haddon (ed.), *International Collaborative Research. Cross-cultural Differences and Cultures of Research*. Brussels: COST, 13–51.

Thompson, R., Kehily, M.J., Hadfield, L. and Sharpe, S. (2009) The making of modern motherhoods: storying an emergent identity. In M. Wetherell (ed.), *Identity in the 21st Century: New Trends in Changing Times*. Basingstoke: Palgrave Macmillan.

Thurlow, C. and McKay, S. (2003) Profiling 'new' communication technologies in adolescence. *Journal of Language and Social Psychology*, 22(1), 94–103.

Tope, A. (2011) Young people's experience of online social network systems in relation to their peer relationships at school. Unpublished MSc dissertation, University of Oxford Department of Education.

Tripp, L.M. (2010) The computer is not for you to be looking around, it is for schoolwork: challenges for digital inclusion as Latino immigrant families negotiate children's access to the Internet. *New Media and Society*, 13(4), 552–67.

Tsatsou, P. (2011) Digital divides revisited: what is new about divides in their research. *Media Culture and Society*, 33(2): 317–31.

Turkle, S. (2010). *Alone Together: Why We Expect More from Technology and Less from Each Other*. New York: Basic Books.

Valckea, M., Bontea, S., De Wevera, B. and Rotsa, I. (2010) Internet parenting styles and the impact on Internet use of primary school children. *Computers and Education*, 55(2), 454–64.

Valentine, G. and Holloway, S.L. (2002) Cyberkids? Exploring children's identities and social networks in on-line and off-line worlds. *Association of American Geographers*, 92, 302–19.

Valkenburg, P., Schouten, A. and Peter, J. (2005). Adolescents' identity experiments on the Internet. *New Media and Society*, 7(3), 383–402.

Vandenbroeck, M., Verschelden, G. and Boonaert, T. (2008) E-learning in a low-status female profession: the role of motivation, anxiety and social support in the learning divide. *Journal of Computer Assisted Learning*, 24(3), 181–90.

Van Deursen, A.J. and van Dijk, J.A. (2009) Improving digital skills for the use of online public information and services. *Government Information Quarterly*, 26(2), 333–40.

Van Rompaey, V., Roe, K. and Struys, K. (2002) Children's influence on Internet access at home: adoption and use in the family context. *Information, Communication and Society*, 5(2), 189–206.

Verdegem, P. and Verhoest, P. (2009) Profiling the non-user: rethinking policy initiatives stimulating ICT acceptance. *Telecommunications Policy*, 33, 642–52.

Warschauer, M., Knobel, M. and Stone, L. (2004) Technology and equity in schooling: deconstructing the digital divide. *Educational Policy*, 18(4), 562–88.

Webster, F. (2006). *Theories of the Information Society*. 3rd edn. London: Routledge.

Wellman, B. and Haythornthwaite, C. (2002). *The Internet in Everyday Life*. Oxford: Blackwell.

Willet, R. (2009) 'It feels like you've grown up a bit': Bebo and teenage identity. The educational and social impact of new technologies on young people in Britain. *Report No. 4*. Available online at: www.education.ox.ac.uk/wordpress/wp-content/uploads/2010/07/Seminar-4-Report.pdf.

Williams, R. and Edge, D. (1996) The Social Shaping of Technology. In W.H. Dutton (ed.), *Information and Communication Technologies: Visions and Realities*. Oxford: Oxford University Press, 37–52.

Wittwer, J. and Senkbeil, M. (2008) Is students computer use at home related to their mathematical performance at school? *Computers and Education*, 50, 1558–71.

Woodfine, B.P., Baptisa Nunes, M. and Wright, D.J. (2008) Text-based synchronous e-learning and dyslexia: not necessarily the perfect match! *Computers and Education*, 50(3), 703–17.

Woolgar, S. (2002) Five rules of virtuality. In S. Woolgar (ed.), *Virtual Society? Technology, Cyberbole, Reality*. Oxford: Oxford University Press, 1–23.

Wyatt, S. (2003) Non-users also matter: the construction of users and non-users of the Internet. In N. Oudshoorn and T. Pinch (eds), *How Users Matter: The Co-Construction of Users and Technologies*. Cambridge, MA: The MIT Press, 67–79.

Wyatt, S., Thomas, G. and Terranova, T. (2002) They came, they surfed, they went back to the beach: conceptualizing use and non-use of the Internet. In S. Woolgar (ed.), *Virtual Society? Technology, Cyberbole, Reality*. Oxford: Oxford University Press, 23–41.

Wyness, M. (2012) *Childhood and Society*. Basingstoke: Palgrave.

Wynn, E. and Katz, J. (1997) Hyperbole over cyberspace: self-presentation and social boundaries in Internet home pages and discourse. *The Information Society*, 13(4), 297–327.

Zelizer, V.A. (1985) *Pricing the Priceless Child: The Changing Social Value of Children*. New York: Basic Books.

Zhao, S. (2009) Parental education and children's online health information seeking: beyond the digital divide debate. *Social Science and Medicine*, 69(10), 1501–5.

Zillien, N. and Hargittai, E. (2009) Digital distinction: status-specific types of Internet usage. *Social Science Quarterly*, 90(2), 274–91.

Zimmer-Gembeck, M.J. and Collins, W.A. (2003) Autonomy development during adolescence. In G.R. Adams and M. Berzonsky (eds), *Blackwell Handbook of Adolescence*. Oxford: Blackwell, 175–204.

Index

Adolescence and Society
Series Editor: John C. Coleman, OBE
Department of Education, University of Oxford

In the 20 years since it began, this series has published some of the key texts in the field of adolescent studies. The series has covered a very wide range of subjects, almost all of them being of central concern to students, researchers and practitioners. A mark of its success is that a number of books have gone to second and third editions, illustrating its popularity and reputation.

The primary aim of the series is to make accessible to the widest possible readership important and topical evidence relating to adolescent development. Much of this material is published in relatively inaccessible professional journals, and the objective of the books has been to summarise, review and place in context current work in the field, so as to interest and engage both an undergraduate and a professional audience.

The intention of the authors is to raise the profile of adolescent studies among professionals and in institutions of higher education. By publishing relatively short, readable books on topics of current interest to do with youth and society, the series makes people more aware of the relevance of the subject of adolescence to a wide range of social concerns.

The books do not put forward any one theoretical viewpoint. The authors outline the most prominent theories in the field and include a balanced and critical assessment of each of these. Whilst some of the books may have a clinical or applied slant, the majority concentrate on normal development.

The readership rests primarily in two major areas: the undergraduate market, particularly in the fields of psychology, sociology and education; and the professional training market, with particular emphasis on social work, clinical and educational psychology, counselling, youth work, nursing and teacher training.

Also in this series:

Teenagers and Technology

D0147409

The popular media often presents a negative picture of young people and technology. From addiction to gaming and the distractions of the Internet to the risks of social networking, the downsides of new technology in the lives of teenagers are often over-blown.

Teenagers and Technology presents a balanced picture of the part played by technology in the lives of young people. Drawing on extensive interviews conducted over several years, this book offers a timely and non-sensational exploration of teenagers' experiences and opinions about the digital technologies they use, desire and dislike.

The book covers a range of topical subjects including:

- social networking and online engagement in the wider social world
- building online self-identity and group membership
- technology in the home
- developing technology skills in support of learning
- drawing on technological resources in the journey towards adulthood.

Grounded in what young people actually say about using new technology in their daily lives, *Teenagers and Technology* explores the unique relationship young people have with digital media, but also draws parallels to how new technology is used throughout society. Importantly, it also discusses the so-called 'digital divide' whereby some teenagers have limited access to new technologies, and the issues that this raises.

By providing a nuanced view on the topic, *Teenagers and Technology* counters the extreme accounts of 'digital youth' and exaggerated anxieties created by the mass media. It will be of interest to students and academics working in the fields of adolescent and Internet studies, along with education professionals, practitioners, teenagers and their parents.

Chris Davies teaches and researches at the University of Oxford, Department of Education. He directed the research project which features in this book and currently runs the Kellogg Centre for Research on Assistive Technologies.

Rebecca Eynon is Research Fellow at the Oxford Internet Institute and Lecturer in Education at the University of Oxford. She is Co-editor of the journal *Learning, Media and Technology* and her research focuses on learning, new technologies, youth and everyday life.